I0698300

DICTIONARY OF 15- TO 18- LETTER WORDS

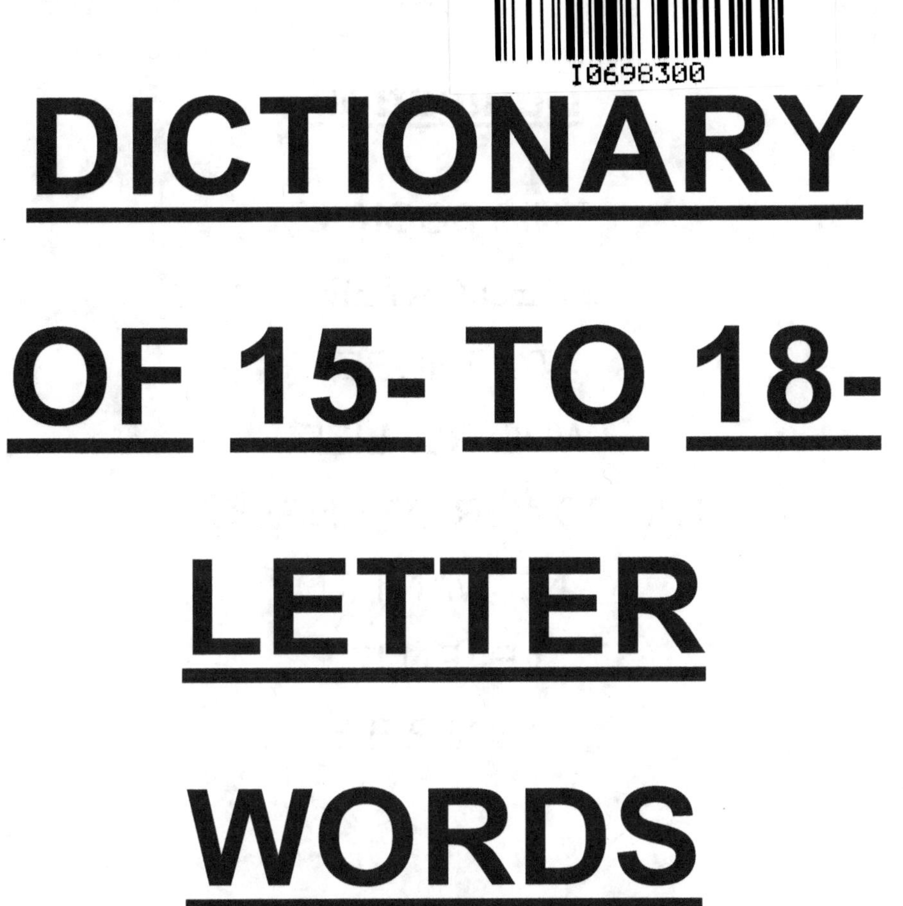

WORDS YOU SHOULD KNOW

MANIK JOSHI

<u>Dedication</u>

THIS BOOK IS

DEDICATED

TO THOSE

WHO REALIZE

THE POWER OF ENGLISH

AND WANT TO

LEARN IT

SINCERELY

<u>Copyright</u> <u>Notice</u>

All rights reserved. Please note that the content in this book is protected under copyright law. This book is for your personal use only. No part of this book may be reproduced, stored in a retrieval system, or transmitted, in any form or by any means, electronic, mechanical, recording, or otherwise, without the prior written permission of the author.

Copyright Holder -- Manik Joshi
License -- Standard Copyright License
Year of Publication – 2021
Email -- manik85joshi@gmail.com

****

<u>IMPORTANT</u> <u>NOTE</u>

This Book is Part of a Series
SERIES Name: "Words by Number of Letters"
[A Ten-Book Series]
BOOK Number: 10
BOOK Title: "Dictionary of 15- to 18-Letter Words"
****

Table of Contents

15- to 18-Letter Words

Letter A -- <u>38</u> 15- to 18-Letter Words
Letter B -- <u>06</u> 15- to 18-Letter Words
Letter C -- <u>88</u> 15- to 18-Letter Words
Letter D -- <u>43</u> 15- to 18-Letter Words
Letter E -- <u>31</u> 15- to 18-Letter Words
Letter F, G -- <u>06</u> 15- to 18-Letter Words
Letter H -- <u>13</u> 15- to 18-Letter Words
Letter I -- <u>188</u> 15- to 18-Letter Words
Letter J, K -- <u>04</u> 15- to 18-Letter Words
Letter L -- <u>04</u> 15- to 18-Letter Words
Letter M -- <u>29</u> 15- to 18-Letter Words
Letter N -- <u>06</u> 15- to 18-Letter Words
Letter O -- <u>17</u> 15- to 18-Letter Words
Letter P -- <u>44</u> 15- to 18-Letter Words
Letter Q -- <u>03</u> 15- to 18-Letter Words
Letter R -- <u>11</u> 15- to 18-Letter Words
Letter S -- <u>33</u> 15- to 18-Letter Words
Letter T -- <u>29</u> 15- to 18-Letter Words
Letter U -- <u>89</u> 15- to 18-Letter Words
Letter V - Z -- <u>01</u> 15- to 18-Letter Words

<u>TOTAL -- 683 Useful 15- to 18-Letter Words</u>

<u>SYMBOLS USED IN THIS DICTIONARY</u>
adj. -- adjective // adv. -- adverb // n. -- noun // prep. -- preposition // pron. -- pronoun // v. -- verb // sb -- somebody // sth -- something

["Letter Count" has been mentioned in the bracket after each and every word.]

<u>15- to 18-Letter Words -- A</u>

1. **absentmindedness** *[16]* [n.] -- a lack of attention or awareness to what you are doing or what is happening around you [*synonym:* inattentiveness]

2. **acclimatization** *[15]* [n.] -- the process of getting used to a new place, situation, environment, climate, weather, temperature, altitude, etc. so that it is not a problem anymore [*synonym:* adaptation]

3. **accommodatingly** *[15]* [adv.] -- in a manner that is characterized by being eager or willing to help or please or do what someone else wants or requests

4. **accountableness** *[15]* [n.] -- the quality or state of being answerable or accountable

5. **acquaintanceship** *[16]* [n.] -- *(a).* a slight knowledge of or familiarity with sth | *(b).* the state of being familiar with sb in a way that involves less intimate relation than friendship

6. **acquisitiveness** *[15]* [n.] -- excessive interest in acquiring and owning money or new possessions (material things) in a greedy way [*synonyms:* covetousness, hoarding, materialism]

7. **acrimoniousness** *[15]* [n.] -- (of an argument, a speech, discussion, behavior, etc.) the fact or quality of having strong bitter, sharp or harsh feelings and words | *(b).* state of having a strong unpleasant taste or smell

8. **administratively** *[16]* [adv.] -- in a way that is connected with organizing or managing the activities or operations of a business, company, institution, organization, government, etc.

9. **advantageousness** *[16]* **[n.]** -- the quality or state of being good, useful, helpful or favorable in a particular situation [*synonym:* profitableness]

10. **adventurousness** *[15]* **[n.]** -- *(a).* the trait of being willing to take risks and try new ideas, methods, things or experiences | *(b).* a state of having full of new, exciting or dangerous ideas, methods, things or experiences [*synonyms:* audaciousness, boldness, daringness]

11. **alphanumerical** *[16]* **[adj.]** -- containing or using letters of the alphabet or numbers and often other symbols or characters such as punctuation marks and mathematical symbols

12. **alphanumerically** *[16]* **[adv.]** -- in a manner that is characterized by containing or using letters of the alphabet or numbers and often other symbols or characters such as punctuation marks and mathematical symbols

13. **ambidextrousness** *[16]* **[n.]** -- the fact or property of being equally skillful with each hand

14. **antagonistically** 16 **[adv.]** -- in a manner that shows or feels dislike or opposition [*synonym:* hostility]

15. **antepenultimate** *[15]* **[adj.]** -- [only before noun] two before the last in a series; third last

16. **anthropocentric** *[15]* **[adj.]** -- believing that humans are the most significant or central entity of the universes

17. **anthropocentricism** *[18]* **[n.]** -- the belief that humans are the most significant or central entity of the universes

18. **anthropomorphic** *[15]* **[adj.]** -- (of beliefs or ideas) treating gods, animals, objects or other non-human entities as having a human form or human qualities

19. **anthropomorphic** *[15]* **[adj.]** -- treating gods, animals or objects as if they have characteristics (in terms of appearance, behavior, etc.) of human beings

20. **anthropomorphism** *[16]* **[n.]** -- the treating of gods, animals, objects or other non-human entities as having a human form or human qualities

21. **anthropomorphism** *[16]* **[n.]** -- treatment of gods, animals or objects as if they have characteristics (in terms of appearance, behavior, etc.) of human beings

22. **antipathetically** *[16]* **[adv.]** -- in a manner that is characterized by showing a strong feeling of dislike for sb/sth

23. **apocalyptically** *[15]* **[adv.]** -- in a manner that relates to, shows, or describes the total destruction of sth, especially of the world

24. **approachability** *[15]* **[n.]** -- the quality or state of being easy to get to [*synonym:* accessibility]

25. **approachableness** *[16]* **[n.]** -- the quality of being friendly and easy to meet, talk to or deal with | (of a place) the quality of being able to be reached from a particular direction or position, or by a particular method. [*synonym:* accessible]

26. **architectonical** *[15]* **[adj.]** -- in a manner that relates to the principles of design and structure

27. **architectonically** *[17]* **[adv.]** -- in a manner that is characterized by having or relating to qualities, such as design and structure, that are considered to be of architectural methods, principles, etc.

28. **architecturally** *[15]* **[adv.]** -- in a manner that is related to the art and practice of designing and constructing buildings

29. **argumentatively** *[16]* **[adv.]** -- in a manner that shows someone wants to argue

30. **argumentativeness** *[17]* **[n.]** -- the state or fact of showing a tendency to argue

31. **aristocratically** *[16]* **[adv.]** -- in a manner that is characterized by having the tastes, manners, or other characteristics of the people of the upper classes

32. **ascertainableness** *[17]* **[n.]** -- the quality of being able to be found out, determined, fixed, etc.

33. **asymptomatically** *[16]* **[adv.]** -- (of a person or illness) in a manner that shows no symptoms

34. **atmospherically** *[15]* **[adv.]** -- *(a).* in a manner that relates to the mixture of gases that surrounds a place, earth, planet, star, etc. | *(b).* in a manner that creates an emotional or thrilling mood

35. **authoritarianism** *[16]* **[n.]** -- the doctrine or principle that does not allow people the personal freedom to decide or act for themselves and forces them to strictly obey authority and rules that may seem unfair

36. **authoritatively** *[15]* **[adv.]** -- *(a).* in a way that shows confidence, control, and expectation to be respected and obeyed [*synonym: commandingly*] | *(b).* in a way that you can trust and respect as true, factual and correct

37. **autobiographical** *[16]* **[adj.]** -- *(a).* based on, marked by, dealing with or involving one's own experiences or life history | *(b).* relating to or in the style of an autobiography

38. **autobiographically** *[18]* **[adv.]** -- *(a).* in a manner that is based on, marked by, dealing with or involving one's own experiences or life history | *(b).* in a manner that relates to or is in the style of an autobiography

<u>15- to 18-Letter Words</u> -- <u>B</u>

1. **bibliographically** *[17]* [adv.] -- in a manner that relates to or is similar to a bibliography, which is a list of the books and articles that a writer referenced or utilized to create a particular book or article

2. **bibliographical** *[15]* [adj.] -- *(a).* relating to a list of books or articles about a specific subject or by a specific author or publisher | *(b).* relating to a list of all of the resources such as articles and books that have been used in the process of researching a work | *(c).* relating to the study of the history of books and their publication or production

3. **biodegradability** *[16]* [n.] -- the fact of breaking down of organic matter to the base substances by microorganisms, such as bacteria and fungi

4. **blasphemousness** *[15]* [n.] -- (of behavior or language) the fact of showing contempt or disrespect for God, deity, religion or holy/sacred objects [*synonym:* irreverence]

5. **broadmindedness** *[15]* [n.] -- the state or quality of being open to new things, ideas or improvements, etc.

6. **bureaucratically** *[16]* [adv.] -- in a manner that is connected with the system of extremely complicated and often unnecessary official rules and ways of doing things that a government or an organization has [*synonyms:* administratively, civically, governmentally, procedurally]

15- to 18-Letter Words -- C

1. **cannibalistically** *[17]* **[adv.]** -- *(a).* in a manner that relates to the practice or behavior of eating the flesh of a human being by another human being | *(b).* in a manner that relates to the practice or behavior of eating the flesh of an animal by the member of its own species

2. **cantankerousness** *[16]* **[n.]** -- the quality of being bad-tempered, quarrelsome, difficult or irritating to handle [*synonym:* crankiness]

3. **carnivorousness** *[15]* **[n.]** -- *(a).* (of an animal) the fact of feeding on the flesh of other animals | *(b).* (of a plant) the fact of being able to trap and digest small creatures such as insects

4. **cartographically** *[16]* **[adv.]** -- in a manner that relates to the art, science, process or practice of drafting, drawing or making maps

5. **catastrophically** *[16]* **[adv.]** -- *(a).* in a manner that involves great destruction, damage or suffering by a sudden event [*synonym:* disastrously] | *(b).* in a manner that involves great difficulty, trouble, disappointment, etc.

6. **ceremoniousness** *[15]* **[n.]** -- the fact of behaving or being performed in an extremely formal, serious or polite way [*synonym:* dignified]

7. **characteristically** *[18]* **[adv.]** -- in a way that highlights the most typical qualities of sb or sth that a person often involves in

8. **charismatically** *[15]* **[adv.]** -- in a manner that shows a lot of attraction, influence, and inspiration

9. **chauvinistically** *[16]* **[adv.]** -- in a way that seems to have an aggressive, unreasonable and enthusiastic belief that your own group, country, etc. is s the best or most important

10. **chemotherapeutic** *[16]* **[adj.]** -- relating to the treatment of a disease, especially cancer by means of chemical substances that stop the growth of cancer cells

11. **chemotherapeutical** *[18]* [adj.] -- relating to the treatment of a disease, especially cancer by means of chemical substances that stop the growth of cancer cells

12. **chronologically** *[15]* [adv.] -- in a way that arranges or lists the order in which a series of events actually occurred

13. **chronometrically** *[16]* [adv.] -- in a manner that relates to the scientific observation of time

14. **cinematographer** *[15]* [n.] -- a person who specializes in the art and methods relating to the shooting of a film that involves shots, lighting, operating a camera, etc.

15. **circumferential** *[15]* [adj.] -- encircling the outside edge of a round or curved area, object, organ, or body part

16. **circumferentially** *[17]* [adv.] -- in a manner that encircles the outside edge of a round or curved area, object, organ, or body part

17. **circumnavigation** *[16]* [n.] -- *(a).* an act of going or moving around sth in order to avoid hitting it | *(b).* an act of sailing, flying or traveling all around sth (especially an island, continent, whole world, planet, etc.) completely in a big circle

18. **circumnavigation** *[16]* [n.] -- *(a).* the action or process of traveling or sailing all the way around the island, continent, world, etc. | *(b).* the action of going around sth in order to avoid an obstacle | *(c).* the action of avoiding a problem, difficulty or unpleasant thing, etc.

19. **circumscription** *[15]* [n.] -- *(a).* the act of limiting or controlling sth such as freedom, rights, activity, range, power | *(b).* an act of drawing a line or circle around another shape

20. **circumstantially** *[16]* [adv.] -- in a manner that relates to, or derived from or is dependent on circumstances

21. **claustrophobic** *[14]* [adj.] -- making you feel abnormally uncomfortable or worried because of being small and closed

22. **claustrophobically** *[18]* [adv.] -- in a way that makes you feel abnormally uncomfortable or worried because of being small and closed

23. **collaboratively** *[15]* [adv.] -- *(a).* in the manner of working together with sb in order to create/produce a particular thing or achieve a particular goal [*synonym:* cooperate] | *(b).* in the manner of working secretly to help the enemy of your country during a war

24. **combustibleness** *[15]* [n.] -- the quality, state or fact of being able to catch fire and burn easily

25. **comfortableness** *[15]* [n.] -- the quality or state of being physically or mentally relaxed and feeling no pain

26. **commemorational** *[15]* [adj.] -- relating to the act or an instance of remembering or memorizing sb/sth

27. **commendableness** *[15]* [n.] -- the quality or state of being worthy of admiration or praise

28. **commercialization** *[17]* [n.] -- the act or fact of managing, using, or exploiting sth and making them available as a commodity to gain profit, especially in a way that other people do not welcome

29. **communicability** *[15]* [n.] -- *(a).* the quality or fact of being able to convey, pass on or communicate to other people | *(b).* (of a disease) the quality or fact of being able to be transmitted from one person or species to another [*synonyms:* catching, contagious, infectious, transmissible]

30. **communicableness** *[16]* [n.] -- *(a).* (of an infectious disease) the quality of being able to be transmitted from one person or animal to another | *(b).* (of a message) the quality of being able to communicate from one person or animal to another

31. **communicational** *[15]* [adj.] -- relating to or characterized by the act or process of using words, sounds, symbols or behaviors to express ideas or exchange information

32. **communicatively** *[15]* **[adv.]** -- in a manner that is characterized by willingness, eagerness, or ability to talk, exchange or impart ideas, information or news

33. **communicativeness** *[17]* **[n.]** -- the quality of being willing, eager, or able to talk, exchange or impart ideas, information or news

34. **companionability** *[16]* **[n.]** -- the fact of being friendly and pleasant to be with [*synonyms:* sociability, unreservedness]

35. **companionableness** *[17]* **[n.]** -- the quality of being close, social and friendly

36. **compartmentalize** *[16]* **[v.]** -- to divide sth into separate sections so that one thing remains affectless with the other

37. **compassionately** *[15]* **[adv.]** -- in a sympathetic way [*synonyms:* benevolently, empathetically, sympathetically]

38. **complimentarily** *[15]* **[adv.]** -- in a manner that expresses praise or admiration for someone or sth

39. **compositionally** *[15]* **[adv.]** -- in a way that combines or arranges the distinct parts or elements to form a whole

40. **comprehensibility** *[17]* **[n.]** -- the state or fact of being possible to be understood [*synonyms:* explicability, intelligibility]

41. **comprehensibleness** *[18]* **[n.]** -- the quality, state or fact of being possible to be understood [*synonym:* intelligibleness]

42. **comprehensively** *[15]* **[adv.]** -- in a manner that includes all, most or many items such as details, facts, information, etc. that are necessary and connected with a particular subject

43. **comprehensiveness** *[17]* **[n.]** -- the state, quality or fact of including all, most or many items such as details, facts, information, etc. that are necessary and connected with a particular subject

44. **computationally** *[15]* **[adv.]** -- *(a).* in a way that relates to the process of mathematical calculation | *(b).* in a way that relates to or involves the use of computers

45. **conceivableness** *[15]* **[n.]** -- the quality or state of being possible to imagine or think of

46. **condescendingly** *[15]* **[adv.]** -- in a manner that shows that you think you are more important or more intelligent than someone else [*synonym:* disdainfully]

47. **configurability** *[15]* **[n.]** -- the state or quality of allowing rearrangement or adjustment

48. **conformableness** *[15]* **[n.]** -- the quality or state of being similar in character, form or nature to sth

49. **confrontational** *[15]* **[adj.]** -- showing the tendency to deal with people or situations in an angry or aggressive way, causing strong arguments, angry disagreements or even a fight

50. **confrontationally** *[17]* **[adv.]** -- tending to deal with or handle situations in an angry or argumentative manner

51. **connoisseurship** *[15]* **[n.]** -- a kind of expertise in a particular subject such as arts, food, drink, etc.

52. **consanguineously** *[16]* **[adv.]** -- in a manner that relates to or involves people of the same blood or origin, descended from the same ancestor

53. **conscientiously** *[15]* **[adv.]** -- in a manner that involves great care, attention [*synonym:* alertly]

54. **conscientiousness** *[17]* **[n.]** -- the quality of wishing to do one's work or duty attentively, correctly, properly and thoroughly [*synonyms:* meticulousness, fussiness]

55. **consequentially** *[15]* **[adv.]** -- in a manner that happens or follows as a result, conclusion, outcome or an effect of a particular event, situation, etc. [*synonym:* resultantly]

56. **consequentially** *[15]* **[adv.]** -- in a manner that is of great importance or significance [*synonym:* inevitably]

57. **conservativeness** *[16]* **[n.]** -- a tendency to preserve or maintain existing conditions, institutions, traditions, etc.

58. **considerateness** *[15]* [n.] -- the state or quality of showing concern about other people's feelings, wishes and needs; the state or quality of showing you are careful not to hurt others' feelings [*synonym:* thoughtfulness]

59. **conspicuousness** *[15]* [n.] -- the quality of being very noticeable or easy to see, especially in a way that is not wanted

60. **conspiratorially** *[16]* [adv.] -- *(a).* in a way that suggests or relates to a group of persons conspiring to do sth wrong, unlawful or harmful or destructive | *(b).* in a manner that suggests the sharing of secret knowledge with another individual

61. **constitutionalism** *[17]* [n.] -- a doctrine that a government's authority is determined or limited by a body of established set of principles or constitution

62. **constitutionally** *[16]* [adv.] -- *(a).* in a manner that relates to the established set of principles of nation, state, organization or group | *(b).* in a manner that is allowed or limited by the established set of principles of a nation, state, organization or group | *(c).* in a manner that relates to the ability of the body or mind to stay fit, healthy and strong

63. **constructiveness** *[16]* [n.] -- the quality of having a useful effect with an intention to help to improve sth

64. **containerization (containerisation)** *[16]* [n.] -- the process of packing and transporting things in containers

65. **contemplatively** *[15]* [adv.] -- in a way that involves quiet and serious thought for a period of time [*synonym:* ponderingly]

66. **contemporaneous** *[15]* [adj.] -- happening, originating, living or existing in the same period of time [*synonyms:* contemporary, simultaneous]

67. **contemporaneously** *[17]* [adv.] -- in a way that is happening, originating, living or existing in the same period of time [*synonyms:* contemporarily, simultaneously]

68. **contemptibility** *[15]* **[n.]** -- the quality or state of not deserving any admiration or respect at all [*synonym:* despicability]

69. **contemptibleness** *[16]* **[n.]** -- the quality or state of not deserving any admiration or respect at all

70. **contemptuousness** *[16]* **[n.]** -- the state of feeling or showing extreme dislike, hatred or disapproval for sb/sth [*synonyms:* disdainfulness, scornfulness]

71. **contentiousness** *[15]* **[n.]** -- the quality or state of being argumentative, irritable or quarrelsome

72. **contextualization (contextualisation)** *[17]* **[v.]** -- the process of taking sth into account in respect to the situation, condition or circumstance in which it happens or exists

73. **contractibleness** *[16]* **[n.]** -- the fact of being able to be shrunk or contract

74. **contradictorily***[15]* **[adv.]** -- in a way that is characterized by a lack of agreement between actions, facts, statements, or opinions, etc. [*synonym:* paradoxically]

75. **controllability** -- 15 **[n.]** -- ability to be affected, directed, influenced or managed

76. **controversially** *[15]* **[adv.]** -- in a manner that creates controversy or intense public disagreement

77. **conventionality** *[15]* **[n.]** -- *(a).* the state or quality of being based on or in accordance with conduct, standards, etc that has been generally accepted, believed, or done in a society for a long time [*synonyms:* orthodoxy, traditionalism] | *(b).* the tendency to follow conduct, standards, etc that is generally accepted, believed, or done in a society and seems to be boring

78. **conversableness** *[15]* **[n.]** -- the quality or state of being easy and pleasant to talk with

79. **conversationalist** *[17]* [n.] -- a person who is skilled at conversing with others, particularly informally

80. **conversationally** *[16]* [adv] -- *(a).* in a manner that is not formal | *(b).* in a manner that relates to, connects with, or is like a conversation

81. **convertibleness** *[15]* [n.] -- the fact of being able to be changed to a different character, form, function, or use: [*synonym:* changeableness]

82. **correspondingly** *[15]* [adv.] -- in a manner that is similar to, or connected with sth in character, form, degree, position or function, etc. [*synonyms:* analogously, equivalently]

83. **corroboratively** *[15]* [adv.] -- in a manner that is characterized by serving to support or establish a statement, theory, or finding by providing information or evidence [*synonym:* confirmatively]

84. **corruptibleness** *[15]* [n.] -- the quality or state of being susceptible to do sth dishonest or immoral

85. **counterfactually** *[16]* [adv.] -- in a manner that is opposed to the facts of an event, situation, circumstance, etc.

86. **creditworthiness** *[16]* [n.] -- the fact of how trustable you are to receive new credit, based on your ability and consistency in paying the money back that was borrowed or owed in the past

87. **criminalization (criminalisation)** [n.] -- an act of making an activity illegal and punishable by passing a new law

88. **customizability** *[15]* [n.] -- ability to be made or changed sth to suit the particular needs of the user

15- to 18-Letter Words -- D

1. **decentralization** *[16]* [n.] -- (of government, organization, etc.) transfer or distribution of some of the administrative powers, authorities, functions or control to several smaller parts, offices, etc. around the country

2. **decipherability** *[15]* [n.] -- ability to make out the meaning of sth that is difficult to read or understand

3. **declassification** *[16]* [n.] -- the action of declaring officially that secret government information, document, report, etc. is no longer secret and the public is allowed to see or learn about it

4. **decomposability** *[15]* [n.] -- the extent, state or quality of breaking into constituent parts or elements

5. **decontamination** *[15]* [n.] -- an act of removing or destroying harmful or dangerous substances from a place, object, or person

6. **decriminalization** *[17]* [n.] -- the action or process of changing the law in order to stop sth from being illegal [*synonym:* legalization]

7. **defenselessness (defencelessness)** *[15]* [n.] -- the state, quality or fact of being too weak to protect yourself, and prone to attack or harm from sb/sth [*synonym:* vulnerability]

8. **delightsomeness** *[15]* [n.] -- the quality or state of having great pleasure

9. **democratization** *[15]* [n.] -- the act or process of making a country, an organization or an institution more independent or self-governing

10. **demographically** *[15]* [adv.] -- in a manner that relates to human populations primarily with respect to their age, gender, births, deaths, diseases, education, marriages, composition, structure and development over a period of time

11. **demonstrability** *[15]* [n.] -- ability to be shown to be true; ability to be proved

12. **demonstrableness** *[16]* **[n.]** -- the quality of being apparent or evident in a clear way, or capable of being proved in a logical way

13. **demonstratively** *[15]* **[adv.]** -- in an open way, showing your feelings of love, affection, etc.

14. **denationalization** *[17]* **[n.]** -- an act or process of transferring ownership of a government organization or an industry to a private company [*synonym:* privatization]

15. **determinability** *[15]* **[n.]** -- the quality of being able to be definitely decided, found out or calculated

16. **developmentally** *[15]* **[adv.]** -- in a manner that is connected with or relates to the process of changing or growing into a more advanced, developed, larger, or more powerful form

17. **diagrammatically** *[16]* **[adv.]** -- in the manner of a graphic representation that is used to show how sth works

18. **differentiation** *[15]* **[n.]** -- *(a).* the action or process of showing, finding or recognizing the difference between two things [*synonym:* demarcation] | *(b).* treatment of people or things in a different and unfair way [*synonym:* discrimination]

19. **disadvantageous** *[15]* **[adj.]** -- creating unfavorable circumstances for sb/sth to succeed or do sth, especially in comparison with other people or things that are getting successful [*synonym:* detrimental]

20. **disadvantageously** *[17]* **[adv.]** -- in a manner that involves creating unfavorable circumstances for sb/sth to succeed or do sth, especially in comparison with other people or things that are getting successful [*synonym:* detrimentally]

21. **disagreeability** *[15]* **[n.]** -- *(a).* the state, quality or fact of not being nice, pleasant, comfortable or enjoyable | *(b).* (of a person) the state, quality or fact of being rude, unhelpful and unfriendly

22. **disagreeableness** *[16]* **[n.]** -- the quality or state of being unpleasant, unfriendly or bad-tempered

23. **disappointingly** *[15]* **[adv.]** -- in a manner that makes you sad or upset because sth did not live up to your expectations in terms of quality, interest, success, etc.

24. **discernibleness** *[15]* **[n.]** -- *(a).* the quality or state of being able to be decided, found out, known, recognized, or understood in spite of not being very noticeable [*synonym:* perceptibility] | *(b).* the quality or state of being able to be seen, smelt or heard through senses with difficulty [*synonym:* distinguishableness]

25. **disconcertingly** *[15]* **[adv.]** -- in a manner that makes sb feel worried, confused or embarrassed, and uncertain

26. **discontinuously** *[15]* **[adv.]** -- *(a).* in a manner that has intervals; in a manner that is characterized by stopping and starting again | *(b).* in a manner that lacks sequence || [*synonyms:* interruptedly, intermittently]

27. **discoverability** *[15]* **[n.]** -- (of information or sth hidden) the quality or fact of being visible, or being possible to find out or make known

28. **discriminatingly** *[16]* **[adv.]** -- in a manner that is characterized by the ability to show good judgment and understanding about the quality of sb/sth [*synonyms:* judiciously, perceptively, sensibly]

29. **disestablishment** *[16]* **[n.]** -- removal of a national Church or other such organized groups from its official status and taking away of official support

30. **dishearteningly** *[15]* **[adv.]** -- in a manner that makes you lose confidence, determination, energy, enthusiasm, courage or hope

31. **dishonorableness** *[16]* **[n.]** -- the quality or state of not deserving admiration, honor or respect [*synonym:* shamefulness]

32. **disinterestedly** *[15]* **[adv.]** -- in a way that is not affected or influenced by personal feelings or the possibility of benefiting yourself in some way [*synonyms:* impartially, neutrally]

33. **disinterestedness** *[17]* **[n.]** -- the quality or state of being impartial; the quality or state of not being involved in a particular event, circumstance or situation

34. **dispassionately** *[15]* [adv.] -- in an unemotional, rational, reasonable and unbiased manner [*synonyms:* impassively, objectively]

35. **disproportionally** *[17]* [adv.] -- in a manner that is not proportional or relative to sth

36. **disproportionate** *[16]* [adj.] -- too large or too small when compared with sth else; out of proportion in amount, size, etc. in comparison with sth else

37. **disproportionately** *[18]* [adv.] -- to an extent that is too large or too small when compared with sth else [*synonyms:* erratically, inconsistently, unduly]

38. **disreputability** *[15]* [n.] -- the fact of being considered to be bad or dishonest in appearance or character [*synonym:* notoriety]

39. **disreputableness** *[16]* [n.] -- the quality or state of lacking respectability reputation, or grace [*synonym:* disreputability]

40. **disrespectfully** *[15]* [adv.] -- in a way that shows a lack of respect for sb/sth

41. **distinctiveness** *[15]* [n.] -- the fact of having a special quality or feature that makes sth clearly different and easily recognizable from other things of the same type [*synonym:* uniqueness]

42. **distinguishable** *[15]* [adj.] -- *(a).* easy to identify or recognize the difference between two persons, animals, or objects, etc. [*synonym:* discernible] | *(b).* possible to be able to see or hear sth

43. **distinguishably** *[15]* [adv.] -- *(a).* in a manner that is easy to identify or recognize the difference between two persons, animals, or objects, etc. [*synonym:* discernible] | *(b).* in a manner that is possible to be able to see or hear sth

15- to 18-Letter Words -- E

1. **ecclesiastically** *[16]* [adv.] -- in a way that is connected with the Christian religion, or to its church leaders or officials

2. **econometrical** *[15]* [adj.] -- relating to the use of statistical and mathematical techniques to assess or evaluate the performance of economies and economic theories

3. **econometrically** *[15]* [adv.] -- in a manner that relates to the use of statistical and mathematical techniques to assess or evaluate the performance of economies and economic theories

4. **efficaciousness** *[15]* [n.] -- (of sth) the property of being capable of producing the effects or results that are desired, intended or wanted, especially of a drug or a medical treatment [*synonym:* effectiveness]

5. **electromagnetic** *[15]* [adj.] -- having electrical characteristics or properties as well as the capacity to draw metal things

6. **electromagnetism** *[16]* [n.] -- the production of an electric current via a magnetic field or a magnetic field via an electric current

7. **enfranchisement** *[15]* [n.] -- the fact of granting a person or group of people the voting right in an election

8. **enthusiastically** *[16]* [adv.] -- in a way that makes it clear that you are intensely excited about sth [*synonyms:* eagerly, earnestly, fervently, passionately]

9. **entomologically** *[15]* [adv.] -- in a manner that relates to insects and their scientific study

10. **entrepreneurial** *[15]* [adj.] -- having the attitude, courage or qualities of an entrepreneur or industrialist; willing to take risks with the intention of making a profit [*synonym:* industrial]

11. **entrepreneurially** *[17]* [adv.] -- in a manner that shows the attitude, courage or qualities of an entrepreneur or industrialist; in a manner that

shows the willingness to take risks with the intention of making a profit [*synonym:* industrially]

12. **entrepreneurship** *[16]* [n.] -- the activity or process of creating a business or businesses, bearing any of its financial risks with an aim to generate profit

13. **environmentalist** *[16]* [n.] -- *(a).* a person who wants to protect the environment from damage by human activities [*synonym:* conservationist] | *(b).* a person who studies the environment or is an expert on environmental problems

14. **environmentally** *[15]* [adv.] -- *(a).* in a manner that is connected with the natural conditions or circumstances under which people, animals, and plants exist.; in a manner that is connected with the environment | *(b).* in a manner that relates to the conditions that affect the behavior, growth and development of sb/sth

15. **epidemiological** *[15]* [adj.] -- relating to the scientific study of the spread and control of diseases

16. **epidemiologically** *[17]* [adv.] -- in a manner that relates to the scientific study of the spread and control of diseases

17. **ethnocentrically** *[16]* [adv.] -- in a manner that relates to a belief that your culture, customs, traditions or ethnic group is superior to another's

18. **ethnographically** *[16]* [adv.] -- in a manner that relates to the qualitative method for collecting data often used in the social and behavioral sciences

19. **euphemistically** *[15]* [adv.] -- in a way that makes sth embarrassing, uncomfortable, humiliating or unpleasant seem more acceptable than it actually is

20. **exceptionableness** *[16]* [n.] -- the quality of being liable to exception, disapproval, objection or opposition

21. **exchangeability** *[15]* **[n.]** -- the quality of involving the act of giving or providing sth to sb and them giving or providing you sb else

22. **exemplification** *[15]* **[n.]** -- the act of giving an example to clarify sth; an example of sth

23. **expeditiousness** *[15]* **[n.]** -- the quality of being quick and attentive to detail without wasting time, money, energy, etc [*synonyms:* celerity, rapidity]

24. **experimentation** *[15]* **[n.]** -- *(a).* the act or process of carrying out a scientific experiment, particularly in a lab, in order to determine sth | *(b).* the action or process of trying out new concepts, ideas, activities or techniques, especially to determine their possible effects

25. **expressionlessly** *[16]* **[adv.]** -- in a way that does not show what sb thinks or feels

26. **extemporization** *[15]* **[n.]** -- (of speech, music, etc.) spoken or performed without thought, planning, practice or preparation

27. **extraordinarily** *[15]* **[adv.]** -- *(a).* in a very unusual, unexpected, strange or remarkable way | *(b).* to a remarkable amount, extent or degree [*synonym:* extremely]

28. **extraterrestrial** *[16]* **[adj.]** -- existing, happening, originating or occurring outside the limits of the earth or its atmosphere [*synonym:* celestial] || **[n.]** -- a creature that comes from another planet or may exist on another planet [*synonym:* alien]

29. **extraterritorial** *[16]* **[adj.]** -- (of a law) valid outside the boundaries or control of a particular country, state, or region where the law was made

30. **extraterritorial** *[16]* **[adj.]** -- located outside the territorial boundaries or jurisdiction of the country

31. **extraterritorially** *[18]* **[adv.]** -- in a manner that is located outside the territorial boundaries or jurisdiction of the country

<u>15-</u> <u>to</u> <u>18-Letter</u> <u>Words</u> -- <u>F, G</u>

1. **familiarization (familiarisation)** *[15]* [n.] -- an act of gaining knowledge or learning about sth and becoming comfortable about it; an act of making sb gain knowledge or learn about sth and become comfortable about it

2. **flirtatiousness** *[15]* [n.] -- (of behavior, actions or individuals) the property of suggesting a sexual interest that is not serious, through comments or actions [*synonym:* playfulness]

3. **gastrointestinal** *[16]* [adj.] -- relating to, including of, or affecting the stomach and intestines

4. **gastronomically** *[15]* [adv.] -- in a manner that is connected with preparing, cooking and eating good and quality food

5. **grandiloquently** *[15]* [adv.] -- (of a person, their language or writing) in a manner that is characterized by using long, complicated or difficult words with an intention to impress people [*synonym:* pompously]

6. **gravitationally** *[15]* [adv.] -- in a way that relates to the force of attraction between two objects

15- to 18-Letter Words -- H

1. **hardheartedness** *[15]* **[n.]** -- an absence of concern, feeling, or compassion for the well-being of others. [*synonym:* heartlessness]

2. **heliocentrically** *[16]* **[adv.]** -- in a manner that has or shows the sun as its central point, as in the accepted astronomical solar system model

3. **hermeneutically** *[15]* **[adv.]** -- in a manner that relates to the meaning of written texts

4. **heterogeneously** *[15]* **[adv.]** -- in a manner that is characterized by the composition of arts, elements, people or things that are unrelated from each other [*synonym:* diversely]

5. **heterogeneousness** *[17]* **[n.]** -- *(a).* the quality or state of being composed of many different, dissimilar, diverse or unrelated elements, ingredients, or parts | *(b).* the property of being not of the same kind or type | (chemistry) denoting a process involving substances in solid, liquid, or gaseous)

6. **homogeneousness** *[15]* **[n.]** -- *(a).* the property of being composed of many same, similar or related elements, ingredients, or parts | *(b).* the property of being of the same kind or type

7. **horticulturalist** *[16]* **[n.]** -- a person who is involved in the study or practice of growing flowers, fruit and vegetables

8. **humanitarianism** *[15]* **[n.]** -- a belief in reducing suffering and improving the living conditions of people

9. **hydrographically** *[16]* **[adv.]** -- connected with the scientific study of the general characteristics of lakes, rivers, and oceans, as well as the production of maps that represent them

10. **hydrostatically** *[15]* **[adv.]** -- in a manner that is concerned with fluids that are not in motion

11. **hypercritically** *[15]* [adv.] -- in a manner that criticizes other people or things too strongly or too often

12. **hypersensitiveness** *[18]* [n.] -- *(a).* the state or quality of being very easily upset or offended [*synonym:* touchiness] | *(b).* the state or quality of being excessively or abnormally, and physically sensitive to light or particular substances, such as medicines, chemicals, etc.

13. **hypochondriacally** *[17]* [adv.] -- in a manner that relates to the condition or state where sb worries constantly about their health yet has no justification for doing so

1. **iconoclastically** *[16]* **[adv.]** -- in a manner that strongly opposes generally accepted beliefs, customs, traditions and opinions

2. **identifiableness** *[16]* **[n.]** -- the quality or state of being able to be recognized

3. **ideographically** *[15]* **[adv.]** -- in a manner that represents ideas by graphic symbols, independently of a particular language, and specific words, phrases or sounds

4. **idiosyncratically** *[17]* **[adv.]** -- in a manner that is characterized by having strange, odd or unusual habits, ways of behaving, or features, etc.

5. **ignominiousness** *[15]* **[n.]** -- the quality or state of being deserved of public embarrassment, shame or humiliation and loss of honor [*synonym:* disgracefulness]

6. **illimitableness** *[15]* **[n.]** -- the quality or state of being without limit or bounds

7. **Illustriousness** *[15]* **[n.]** -- the fact of being very famous or popular, and much admired, especially because of your great achievement(s). [*synonyms:* eminence, reputation, recognition]

8. **immeasurability** *[15]* **[n.]** -- the quality or state of being impossible to assess, determine, calculate, etc. because of the extremely vast size

9. **immeasurableness** *[16]* **[n.]** -- the quality or state of being so large or great that it cannot be measured or known precisely

10. **immunologically** *[15]* **[adv.]** -- in a manner that relates to the scientific study of protection against disease

11. **impenetrability** *[15]* **[n.]** -- *(a).* the quality or state of being impossible to be entered, pierced, passed through or seen through [*synonym:* impassability] | *(b).* the quality or state of being impossible to understand [*synonym:* incomprehensibility]

12. **impenetrableness** *[16]* [n.] -- the quality of being impassable or inaccessible

13. **imperceptibility** *[16]* [n.] -- the quality, state or fact of being extremely slight or small and therefore impossible or very difficult to be seen or felt, or affect the senses

14. **imperceptibleness** *[17]* [n.] -- the quality of being so slight or gradual that cannot be detectable or distinguishable by a sense or by the mind

15. **imperishability** *[15]* [n.] -- the quality of being able to last for a long time or forever without becoming weak, bad or poor

16. **imperishableness** *[16]* [n.] -- the quality or state of being not subject to decay/decompose or come to an end

17. **impermeableness** *[15]* [n.] -- the quality or state of not permitting liquid or gas to go through

18. **impermissibility** *[16]* [n.] -- the fact of being not permissible

19. **imperturbability** *[16]* [n.] -- the quality of being not easily angered, upset or worried by problematic or difficult situations

20. **imperturbability** *[16]* [n.] -- the quality or state of staying calm and controlled in spite of dangers, difficulties or problems

21. **imperturbableness** *[17]* [n.] -- the quality or state of staying calm and controlled without getting affected by problems or difficulties

22. **implicationally** *[15]* [adv.] -- in a manner that relates to or is concerned with the possible effect, impact or result of an action or a decision

23. **imponderability** *[15]* [n.] -- the quality or state of being unable to be determined, evaluated or weighed with exactness

24. **imponderableness** *[18]* [n.] -- the quality of being difficult or impossible to estimate, guess or assess

25. **impracticability** *[16]* [n.] -- (of a course of action) the fact of being impossible or extremely difficult to carry out or be put into practice

26. **impracticableness** *[17]* [n.] -- the quality or state of being unable to be implemented or operable

27. **impressionability** *[17]* **[n.]** -- the quality or state of being easily impressed or influenced

28. **impressionableness** *[18]* **[n.]** -- the quality of being easily impressed or influenced by other people

29. **impressionistic** *[15]* **[adj.]** -- giving a general idea or view rather than particular facts or details

30. **inaccessibility** *[15]* **[n.]** -- *(a).* the quality, state or fact of being difficult or impossible to reach or to get [*synonym:* inapproachability] | *b).* (of language or artistic work) the quality, state or fact of being not easy to understand or appreciate

31. **inaccessibleness** *[16]* **[n.]** -- the quality or state of being difficult or impossible to reach or access

32. **inadmissibility** *[15]* **[n.]** -- the quality, state or fact of being unable to be accepted or allowed, esp. in a court of law [*synonym:* prohibition]

33. **inapplicability** *[15]* **[n.]** -- the fact of being not intended, suitable or relevant for, or directed at sb or sth

34. **inapplicableness** *[16]* **[n.]** -- the quality or state of being irrelevant or unsuitable

35. **inappropriately** *[15]* **[adv.]** -- in a manner that is not suitable, fitting, proper or correct in a particular situation, place, or circumstance, etc. [*synonym:* unsuitably]

36. **inappropriateness** *[17]* **[n.]** -- the fact of not being suitable, fitting, proper or correct in a particular situation, place, or circumstance, etc. [*synonyms:* incongruity, unsuitability]

37. **inarticulateness** *[16]* **[n.]** -- *(a).* (of people) the state, quality or fact of being unable to express ideas, opinions, thoughts, emotions or feelings clearly, easily or effectively [*synonym:* incoherence] | *(b).* (of speech)) the state, quality or fact of not using clear or normal words and therefore difficult to understand

38. **inauspiciousness** *[16]* **[n.]** -- the quality of suggesting that sth will not be successful or positive in the future

39. **incalculability** *[15]* **[n.]** -- the fact of being extremely large or very numerous to evaluate, compute, etc.

40. **incalculableness** *[16]* **[n.]** -- the quality of being too large or great to be calculated, measured or estimated

41. **incombustibility** *[16]* **[n.]** -- the quality or state of being fireproof]

42. **incombustibleness** *[17]* **[n.]** -- the quality, state or fact of being not able to catch fire and burn easily

43. **incommensurability** *[18]* **[n.]** -- the state or quality of being unable to be measured or compared by the same or common basis, standard or measure

44. **incommensurable** *[15]* **[adj.]** -- (of two things) so completely different from each other that they cannot be compared or judged by the same standards, bases or measures

45. **incommensurable** *[15]* **[adj.]** -- that cannot be measured or compared by the same or common basis, standard or measure

46. **incommensurably** *[15]* **[adv.]** -- in a manner that involves the inability to be measured or compared by the same standard or measure

47. **incommensurately** *[16]* **[adv.]** -- in a manner that is characterized by being out of keeping or proportion with sth in size, importance, quality, etc. [*synonyms:* disproportionately, unequally]

48. **incommunicability** *[17]* **[n.]** -- the state or quality of being unable to be communicated, imparted, shared, etc.

49. **incommunicableness** *[18]* **[n.]** -- the quality of being inexpressible or beyond description

50. **incomparability** *[15]* **[n.]** -- the state of being unequal in quality or extent, etc. [*synonym:* matchless]

51. **incomparableness** *[16]* **[n.]** -- the quality of being so good that nothing else can match up [*synonym:* uniqueness]

52. **incompatibility** *[15]* **[n.]** -- *(a).* (of two or more actions, things ideas, etc.) the fact of being so different that they cannot be used, mixed or exist, etc. together because of basic differences | *(b).* (of two people)

the fact of being so different from each other that they can't be able to live or work happily together | *(c).* (of a thing or person) the fact of being not reliable or able to coexist with another | [*synonym:* incongruity]

53. **incompatibleness *[16]* [n.]** -- the quality or state of not deserving any admiration or respect at all

54. **incomprehensible *[16]* [adj.]** -- that is impossible or extremely difficult to be understood [*synonyms:* inexplicable, unfathomable, unintelligible]

55. **incomprehensibly *[16]* [adv.]** -- in a manner that is impossible or extremely difficult to be understood [*synonyms:* inexplicably, unfathomably, unintelligibly]

56. **incomprehension *[15]* [n.]** -- the state of being unable to understand sb/sth

57. **incompressibility *[17]* [n.]** -- the quality or state of being unable to be compressed or condensed

58. **inconceivability *[16]* [n.]** -- the state of being impossible to imagine or think of

59. **inconceivableness *[17]* [n.]** -- the quality of being unthinkable, unimaginable, mind-blowing or beyond belief

60. **incongruousness *[15]* [n.]** -- the quality of being inappropriate, incompatible and unsuitable

61. **inconsequential *[15]* [adj.]** -- not important or worth considering; of little or no value [*synonym:* trivial]

62. **inconsequential *[15]* [adj.]** -- of little or no importance or significance [*synonym:* trivial]

63. **inconsequentially *[17]* [adv.]** -- in a manner that is not important or worth considering; in a manner that is of little or no value [*synonym:* trivially]

64. **inconsequentially *[17]* [adv.]** -- in a manner that is of little or no importance or significance [*synonym:* trivially]

65. **inconsiderableness *[18]* [n.]** -- the quality of being very small in size, amount, or extent and thus appearing unimportant

66. **inconsiderately** *[15]* [adv.] -- in a manner that is characterized by not caring about other people or their feelings, rights or needs [*synonym:* thoughtlessly]

67. **inconsiderateness** *[17]* [n.] -- the quality of not worrying about other people's feelings, emotions or needs [*synonym:* thoughtlessness]

68. **inconsolability** *[15]* [n.] -- the state of being so sad or disappointed that nothing can comfort you or make feel you better

69. **inconsolableness** *[16]* [n.] -- the quality or state of being Impossible or difficult to make sb feel better

70. **inconspicuously** *[15]* [adv.] -- in a manner that is not easily or readily noticed or seen; in a way that is not attracting attention [*synonyms:* ordinarily, unobtrusively, unremarkably]

71. **inconspicuousness** *[17]* [n.] -- the quality of being not easily or readily noticed or seen [*synonyms:* ordinariness, unobtrusiveness]

72. **incontestability** *[16]* [n.] -- the state of being true and therefore cannot be disagreed with, disputed or denied

73. **incontestableness** *[17]* [n.] -- the quality of being impossible to argue about or disagree with

74. **incontrovertible** *[16]* [adj.] -- being obviously true and cannot be disagreed with, disputed, questioned or denied [*synonyms:* indisputable, undeniable, unquestionable]

75. **incontrovertibly** *[16]* [adv.] -- in a manner that is obviously true and cannot be disagreed with, disputed, questioned or denied [*synonyms:* indisputably. undeniably, unquestionably]

76. **incorrigibility** *[15]* [n.] -- (relating to a person or their behavior) the quality, state or fact of having bad habits or faults which cannot be changed, corrected, reformed or improved [*synonym:* incurability]

77. **incorrigibleness** *[16]* [n.] -- (relating to a person or their behavior) the quality, state or fact of having bad habits or faults which cannot be changed, corrected, reformed or improved [*synonym:* incurability]

78. **incorruptibleness** *[17]* [n.] -- the quality, state or fact of not being susceptible to do sth dishonest or immoral

79. **incredulousness** *[15]* [n.] -- the state or quality of being unable to believe sth because it is extremely surprising or shocking [*synonym:* incredulity]

80. **indecipherability** *[17]* [n.] -- the quality or state of being unable to be read or understood [*synonym:* illegibility]

81. **indefatigableness** *[17]* [n.] -- the quality of being always determined and enthusiastic to achieve your goal and never willing to admit defeat

82. **indefeasibility** *[15]* [n.] -- the quality or state of being not liable to be lost, voided, resisted, undone or overturned, etc. [*synonym:* invincibility]

83. **indefensibleness** *[16]* [n.] -- *(a).* the quality, state or fact of not being able to be maintained as right, justified or valid | *(b).* the quality, state or fact of not being able to be protected against physical attack [*synonyms:* unprotected, vulnerability]

84. **indefinableness** *[15]* [n.] -- the quality or state of being impossible to describe, express or explain clearly

85. **indemnification** *[15]* [n.] -- the act of protecting someone from being held legally accountable for their deeds

86. **indestructibility** *[17]* [n.] -- the quality, state or fact of being very strong and almost impossible to be destroyed, broken, or ruined, etc. [*synonyms:* durability, eternality, imperishability]

87. **indestructibleness** *[18]* [n.] -- the quality, state or fact of not being able to be destroyed or damaged

88. **indeterminately** *[15]* [adv.] -- in a manner that cannot be identified, counted or measured easily, exactly or accurately

89. **indigestibility** *[15]* [n.] -- the state of being very difficult or impossible for the stomach to break down the food - that has been eaten - into smaller forms that can be absorbed by the body

90. **indigestibleness** *[16]* [n.] -- *(a).* the quality, state or fact of not being able to be easily digested | *(b).* (of ideas, opinions, etc.) the quality, state or fact of being difficult to understand or figure out

91. **indiscriminately** *[16]* [adv.] -- (of an action) in a manner that doesn't show careful thought about the possible harmful or damaging effects

92. **indispensability** *[16]* [n.] -- the quality or state of being absolutely necessary or crucial

93. **indispensableness** *[17]* [n.] -- the quality or state of being absolutely necessary or crucial

94. **indisputability** *[15]* [n.] -- the quality of being beyond question, disagreement, denial or doubt

95. **indisputableness** *[16]* [n.] -- the quality of being obviously clear, true, or certain

96. **indistinguishable** *[17]* [adj.] -- (of two things) so similar that it is impossible to see any differences between them [*synonym:* identical]

97. **indistinguishably** *[17]* [adv.] -- in a manner that is impossible to judge as being different on comparing to another similar thing

98. **indomitableness** *[15]* [n.] -- the quality or state of being so strong, brave, tough, determined, etc. that it can't be defeated or frightened

99. **indubitableness** *[15]* [n.] -- the quality or state of being unable to be doubted or questioned

100. **industriousness** *[15]* [n.] -- the quality of being hard-working or diligent

101. **inequitableness** *[15]* [n.] -- the quality of being partial, unfair, or unjust

102. **inexcusableness** *[15]* [n.] -- the quality or state of being Impossible to excuse, forgive or justify

103. **inexhaustibility** *[16]* [n.] -- the quality or state of being unable to be completely used up or finished because having in large quantity or amount

104.   **inexhaustibleness** *[17]* **[n.]** -- the quality, state or fact of being unable to be completely used up or finished because having in large quantity or amount

105.   **inexplicability** *[15]* **[n.]** -- the quality of being impossible to interpret or put in plain words

106.   **inexplicableness** *[16]* **[n.]** -- the quality of being unable to be explained or understood

107.   **inexpressibility** *[16]* **[n.]** -- the quality or state of being Impossible to express

108.   **inexpressibleness** *[17]* **[n.]** -- the quality, state or fact of being Impossible to express

109.   **inextensibility** *[15]* **[n.]** -- the quality, state or fact of being unable to be stretched or drawn out to make it bigger or longer

110.   **inextinguishable** *[16]* **[adj.]** -- unable to be put to end from burning or existing [*synonym:* unquenchable]

111.   **inextinguishably** *[16]* **[adv.]** -- in a manner that is unable or impossible to be stopped from burning or existing

112.   **inextricability** *[15]* **[n.]** -- the quality of being linked so closely in a manner that cannot be separated

113.   **inextricableness** *[16]* **[n.]** -- the quality or state of being unable to be divided, separated, freed, or escaped from

114.   **infinitesimally** *[15]* **[adv.]** -- to an extremely small degree

115.   **inflammableness** *[15]* **[n.]** -- the quality or state of being capable of setting on fire easily

116.   **inhospitableness** *[16]* **[n.]** -- the quality or state of being unwelcoming or unfriendly

117.   **injudiciousness** *[15]* **[n.]** -- the quality, state or fact of not showing sensible or wise judgment; the quality, state or fact of being inappropriate in a particular situation [*synonym:* foolishness]

118.	**inquisitorially** *[15]* **[adv.]** -- in a manner that relates to a legal process in which the court investigates the facts before making a judgment

119.	**inseparableness** *[15]* **[n.]** -- the quality of being indivisible or always together

120.	**insignificantly** *[15]* **[adv.]** -- in a manner that is small or unnoticeable, and therefore not important enough to be worth considering

121.	**inspirationally** *[15]* **[adv.]** -- in a manner that encourages sb and makes them feel full of hope

122.	**instantaneously** *[15]* **[adv.]** -- in a manner that happens or is done without delay [*synonym:* immediately]

123.	**instantaneousness** *[17]* **[n.]** -- the quality of being done or occurring immediately and very quickly

124.	**institutionalized** *[17]* **[adj.]** -- *(a).* that has been occurring or being practiced for so long that it is accepted as normal | *(b).* (of people) lacking the ability to live and think without being influenced or controlled because they have spent so long in an institution

125.	**instructionally** *[15]* **[adv.]** -- in a manner that provides information about how to do or use sth

126.	**insubordinately** *[15]* **[adv.]** -- (of a person or behavior) in a manner that is characterized by not obeying rules and orders or showing respect for sb who is in authority [*synonyms:* defiantly, disobediently]

127.	**insubordination** *[15]* **[n.]** -- the act of refusing to obey rules and orders or show respect for sb who is in authority [*synonyms:* defiance, disobedience, noncompliance]

128.	**insubstantially** *[15]* **[adv.]** -- in a way that is not very large, strong important [*synonym:* weakly]

129.	**insufferableness** *[16]* **[n.]** -- the quality or state of being so annoying, unpleasant or uncomfortable, that it can't be tolerated

130.   **insuperableness *[15]* [n.]** -- (of a problem) the quality of being so great or severe that it cannot be defeated, negotiated, or dealt with successfully

131.   **insupportableness *[17]* [n.]** -- the quality of being unable to be supported or justified | the quality of being unable to be endured or bearable

132.   **insurrectionary *[15]* [adj.]** -- (of a large group of people) trying to violently take control of the government [*synonym:* rebellious]

133.   **intellectualism *[15]* [n.]** -- the ability to think about or discuss a subject or topic thoroughly and intelligently, without involving your emotions, sentiments or feelings

134.   **intelligibility *[15]* [n.]** -- (of speech and writing) the quality of being easily and clearly understood [*synonym:* comprehensibility]

135.   **intelligibleness *[16]* [n.]** -- the quality, state or fact of being very easy to understand or comprehend [*synonyms:* comprehensibility, coherence]

136.   **intensification *[15]* [n.]** -- the act of making or becoming greater, stronger, or more extreme [*synonyms:* amplification, escalation, strengthening]

137.   **interchangeability *[18]* [n.]** -- the ability that two objects can be put or used in the place of each other, without making any difference, without affecting their functioning or without being noticed [*synonym:* exchangeability]

138.   **interchangeability *[18]* [n.]** -- the quality or state of being able to be replaced with each other without making any difference or without being noticed

139.   **interchangeable *[15]* [adj.]** -- that can be put or used in the place of each other, without making any difference, without affecting their functioning or without being noticed [*synonym:* exchangeable]

140.   **interchangeably *[15]* [adv.]** -- in a manner that can be put or used in the place of each other, without making any difference, without

affecting their functioning or without being noticed [*synonym:* exchangeable]

141. **intercommunication** *[18]* **[n.]** -- the process of communicating between people or groups or people

142. **interconnectedness** *[18]* **[n.]** -- the state of being connected with each other

143. **intercontinental** *[16]* **[adj.]** -- existing, occurring, traveling, conducted between, or involving two or more continents [*synonyms:* global, worldwide]

144. **interdepartmental** *[17]* **[adj.]** -- existing, occurring, conducted between, or involving two or more departments, especially in a business, academic institution or government, etc.

145. **interdependence** *[15]* **[n.]** -- the quality or condition of two or more objects, individuals or groups being dependent on each other for mutual benefit

146. **interdependency** *[15]* **[n.]** -- the quality or condition of two or more objects, individuals or groups depending on each other

147. **interdependently** *[16]* **[adv.]** -- in a manner that depends on each other, or comprises groups or parts that depend on each other

148. **interdisciplinary** *[17]* **[adj.]** -- existing, occurring, conducted between, or involving two or more branches of knowledge [*synonyms:* global, worldwide]

149. **intergenerational** *[17]* **[adj.]** -- existing, occurring, conducted among, or involving several generations or age categories

150. **intergovernmental** *[17]* **[adj.]** -- existing, occurring, conducted between, or involving two or more governments or divisions of a government

151. **interminability** *[15]* **[n.]** -- the quality of lasting for so long a time that it becomes boring or annoying [*synonym:* endless]

152. **interminableness** *[16]* **[n.]** -- the quality of being continuing for so long time that it becomes boring or irritating

153.   **internationalism** *[16]* **[n.]** -- a political principle that supports or encourages greater political or economic cooperation between or among nations

154.   **internationalize (internationalise)** *[16]* **[v.]** -- to bring sth under the control, power or protection of many countries; to become or make sth become international

155.   **internationally** *[15]* **[adv.]** -- in a manner that involves more than one country or occurs between or among nations [*synonym:* globally]

156.   **interoperability** *[16]* **[n.]** -- the ability of two or more components or systems to exchange information and use it

157.   **interpenetration** *[16]* **[n.]** -- an act of spreading completely in all directions through sth or from one thing to another

158.   **interpersonally** *[15]* **[adv.]** -- in a manner that relates to, or involves relations between persons

159.   **interpretability** *[16]* **[n.]** -- the quality of being able to be understood or explained in plain words

160.   **interpretatively** *[16]* **[adv.]** -- in a manner that relates to explanation, performance or understanding of the meaning of sth

161.   **interrelatedness** *[16]* **[n.]** -- the state of being related or connected with each other

162.   **interrelationship** *[17]* **[n.]** -- the way in which each of two or more things or people are closely related to the others

163.   **interrogatively** *[15]* **[n.]** -- in a manner that is in the form of a question

164.   **interrogatorily** *[15]* **[adv.]** -- in a manner that conveys or expresses a question

165.   **intractableness** *[15]* **[n.]** -- the quality or state of being not easily directed, governed or managed

166.   **intramuscularly** *[15]* **[adv.]** -- in a manner that is located or occurring within a muscle

167.   **invulnerability** *[15]* [n.] -- capability of not being harmed, damaged or defeated [*synonym:* imperviousness]

168.   **invulnerableness** *[16]* [n.] -- the quality of being Immune to attack, harm or damage

169.   **irreclaimableness** *[17]* [n.] -- the quality of being not able to be reclaimed or reformed

170.   **irreconcilability** *[17]* [n.] -- *(a).* (of differences or disagreements) the quality of being too great to be settled | *(b).* (of two ideas or opinions) the quality of being impossible to exist together | *(c).* (of people) the quality of disagreeing with one another

171.   **irreconcilableness** *[18]* [n.] -- the quality or state of being so incompatible, opposed or conflicting that agreement is impossible

172.   **Irrecoverableness** *[17]* [n.] -- the quality or state of not being able to be recovered or regained

173.   **irredeemableness** *[16]* [n.] -- the quality or state of being impossible to change, correct or improve

174.   **irreducibleness** *[15]* [n.] -- the quality, state or fact of being unable to be made smaller or simpler in amount, size, form, etc.

175.   **Irreligiousness** *[15]* [n.] -- the quality, state or fact of being neglectful of or opposed to religion; the quality, state or fact of having not any religious belief; the quality, state or fact of showing no respect or lack of respect for religion [*synonym:* profaneness]

176.   **irremediableness** *[16]* [n.] -- the state or quality of being beyond repair

177.   **irreparableness** *[16]* [n.] -- the quality of being impossible to be repaired or made right again

178.   **irrepressibility** *[16]* [n.] -- *(a).* (of a person) the fact of being happy, lively, enthusiastic and energetic [*synonym:* ebullience] | *(b).* (of feelings, etc.) the quality or state of being impossible to be controlled, restrained or stopped

179.   **irrepressibleness** *[17]* [n.] -- the quality, state or fact of being so lively and energetic that it cannot be repressed, stopped controlled or restrained

180.   **irreproachability** *[17]* [n.] -- the quality or state of being completely blameless or flawless

181.   **irreproachableness** *[18]* [n.] -- the quality of being blameless, faultless in every respect

182.   **irreproducibility** *[17]* [n.] -- the quality, state or fact of being impossible to reproduce or duplicate

183.   **irresistibleness** *[16]* [n.] -- the quality, state or fact of being so powerful or strong that it is impossible to be resisted or opposed

184.   **irresponsibleness** *[17]* [n.] -- the quality, state or fact of having no sense of responsibility or accountability

185.   **irretrievability** *[16]* [n.] -- the state or quality of being difficult or impossible to recover or repair

186.   **irretrievableness** *[17]* [n.] -- the quality of being unable to be repaired, reversed or recovered

187.   **irreversibleness** *[16]* [n.] -- the quality, state or fact of being impossible to change or return to a previous condition

188.   **irrevocableness** *[15]* [n.] -- the quality or state of being Impossible to cancel, change or retract

15- to 18-Letter Words -- J, K

1. **journalistically** *[16]* [adv.] -- in a manner that relates to or is typical of the work of people who write about news
2. **jurisprudential** *[15]* [adj.] -- connected with the science or philosophy of law
3. **jurisprudentially** *[17]* [adv.] -- with regard to the science, study or philosophy of law and the principles on which law is based
4. **knowledgeableness** *[17]* [n.] -- the state, quality, or measure of being well-informed or educated

15- to 18-Letter Words -- L

1. **lackadaisically** *[15]* [adv.] -- in a manner that doesn't show enough care, determination, effort, enthusiasm or interest [*synonym:* apathetically]
2. **lightheadedness** *[15]* [n.] -- a feeling that you are about to faint [*synonym:* dizziness]
3. **lightheartedness** *[16]* [n.] -- the quality or state of being joyful, amused, and carefree, etc.
4. **logarithmically** *[15]* [adv.] -- in a way that relates to a logarithm (= a figure indicating the number of times a given number must be multiplied by itself to yield another number)

15- to 18-Letter Words -- M

1. **magnanimousness** *[15]* [n.] -- the quality of being marked by the strong principles of kindness, generosity, and forgiveness, especially towards your enemy or a competitor/rival [*synonym:* high-mindedness]

2. **maintainability** *[15]* [n.] -- the quality of being able to be continued, supported, etc. at the same level, standard, etc.

3. **maladministration** *[17]* [n.] -- the fact of managing a business, organization or system poorly or dishonestly

4. **maneuverability** *[15]* [n.] -- the quality of being easy to move and direct into different positions

5. **marginalization (marginalisation)** *[15]* [n.] -- the act of giving sb the impression that they are unimportant and powerless to influence decisions or events; to put sb in a position of helplessness and powerlessness

6. **materialization** *[15]* [n.] -- *(a).* the action of actually happening or becoming real in an expected or planned manner | *(b).* an occasion when a ghost, spirit, etc. appears in bodily form in a sudden or unexplainable manner; an occasion when sb/sth appears suddenly and unexpectedly

7. **mechanistically** *[15]* [adv.] -- in a manner that is characterized by treating all living things and natural processes like machines

8. **melancholically** *[15]* [adv.] -- in a manner that feels, causes or expresses sadness, especially for a long time and in a way that cannot be explained

9. **mellifluousness** *[15]* [n.] -- (of music, sound or voice) the property of being pleasingly sweet and smooth or very pleasant to listen to

10. **melodramatically** *[16]* **[adv.]** -- in a manner that involves behaving or showing emotions or excitements in an extreme, unusual and exaggerated way [*synonyms:* histrionically, theatrically]

11. **merchantability** *[15]* **[n.]** -- the quality or state of being suitable for trading (buying and selling)

12. **meteorologically** *[16]* **[adv.]** -- in a manner that relates to weather conditions or forecasting

13. **microbiological** *[15]* **[adj.]** -- relating to the scientific study of very small organisms, such as bacteria, viruses, etc.

14. **microbiologically** *[17]* **[adv.]** -- in a manner that relates to the scientific study of very small organisms, such as bacteria, viruses, etc.

15. **microscopically** *[15]* **[adv.]** -- in a manner that uses or can only be seen with a microscope; in a manner that is done by looking at details very carefully

16. **misanthropically** *[16]* **[adv.]** -- in a manner that is characterized by disliking people and avoiding social situations

17. **misapprehension** *[15]* **[n.]** -- a mistaken belief or wrong idea/understanding about sth. [*synonyms:* misconception, misinterpretation]

18. **misappropriation** *[16]* **[n.]** -- an act of taking sb else's money, property or other belongings for yourself in an unfair or deceitful manner, breaching their trust [*synonym:* embezzlement]

19. **miscellaneously** *[15]* **[adv.]** -- in a manner that includes many things of different kinds

20. **mischievousness** *[15]* **[n.]** -- *(a).* the trait of enjoying playing tricks and causing harm or trouble to people [*synonyms:* impish, naughty, playful] |

(b). the fact or trait of causing or intended to cause harm, trouble or annoyance

21. **misconstruction** *[15]* [n.] -- a completely wrong understanding of sth such as intentions, actions, evidence, facts, etc.

22. **misinterpretation** *[17]* [n.] -- failure to understand or explain wrongly or incorrectly [*synonyms:* misconstrue, misread]

23. **monochromatically** *[17]* [adv.] -- in a manner that contains or uses only one color

24. **monopolistically** *[16]* [adv.] -- in a manner that attempts to fully control or dominate anything, especially an industry or business

25. **monosyllabically** *[16]* [adv.] -- in a way that involves saying very little and rudely or unfriendly

26. **morphologically** *[15]* [adv.] -- in a manner that is characterized by the science of the form and structure of plants, animals, and other organisms

27. **multidisciplinary** *[17]* [adj.] -- involving several different subjects, fields or branches of study

28. **multifariousness** *[16]* [n.] -- the quality of being made of many different elements, individuals, parts, types, or varieties [*synonym:* diversity]

29. **multimillionaire** *[16]* [n.] -- a person with assets and money worth millions of dollars, pounds, etc.

<u>15- to 18-Letter Words -- N</u>

1. **nationalistically** *[17]* **[adv.]** -- in a manner that relates to or shows a belief that your nation is better and more important than other nations

2. **naturalistically** *[16]* **[adv.]** -- in a way that shows things as they really are and not looking artificial

3. **neurotransmitter** *[16]* **[n.]** -- any of a group of chemical substances released by neurons that transmits messages between neurons or between neurons and muscles

4. **noninterventionist** *[18]* **[adj.]** -- favoring the principle of not interfering in the affairs of other nations || **[n.]** -- a supporter of the principle of not interfering in the affairs of other nations

5. **nontraditionally** *[16]* **[adv.]** -- in a manner that is different from the usual customs or traditions

6. **notwithstanding** *[15]* **[prep.]** -- without being affected by sth || **[adv.]** -- however, nevertheless; despite this

<u>15- to 18-Letter Words -- O</u>

1. **objectification** *[15]* **[n.]** -- the act of treating people as if they are objects or things rather than human beings, without feelings, opinions, or rights of their own

2. **observationally** *[15]* **[adv.]** -- in a manner that is related to the act of making and recording a measurement

3. **obstreperousness** *[16]* **[n.]** -- the quality of being difficult to control or deal with, aggressive and noisy

4. **ophthalmologist** *[15]* **[n.]** -- a specialist doctor who studies and treats the disorders and diseases of the eye

5. **opportunistically** *[17]* **[adv.]** -- in a manner that uses a situation to get power or an advantage

6. **organizationally** *[16]* **[adv.]** -- in a way that considers the arrangement of component parts of sth; in a manner that relates to the planning or preparation of an activity or an event

7. **orthographically** *[16]* **[adv.]** -- in a manner that is related to how words are typically spelled and written

8. **overconcentration** *[17]* **[n.]** -- the state or an instance of having things or people in excess

9. **overconfidently** *[15]* **[adv.]** -- in a manner that has or shows too much confidence

10. **overconsumption** *[15]* **[n.]** -- the action, situation or fact of consuming sth too often or too much

11. **overdevelopment** *[18]* **[n.]** -- the state or quality of being developed too much that may have a negative effect on society or the environment

12. **overemotionally** *[15]* **[adv.]** -- in a manner that is characterized by having feelings that are too strong, or expressing feelings too strongly

13. **overenthusiastic** *[16]* **[adj.]** -- having, feeling or showing intense excitement about sth in a manner that seems inappropriate or unreasonable [*synonym:* obsessive]

14. **overgeneralization** *[18]* **[n.]** -- the fact of making a statement or drawing a conclusion that is inaccurate or unjustified because it is excessively general

15. **overindulgently** *[15]* **[adv.]** -- in a manner that allows sb to have more of sth enjoyable or pleasant than is good for them

16. **overrepresented** *[15]* **[adj.]** -- represented in excessively, unreasonably or disproportionately large numbers or amounts

17. **overstimulation** *[15]* **[n.]** -- the quality or fact of becoming too active, interested or excited

<u>15- to 18-Letter Words -- P</u>

1. **paradigmatically** *[16]* **[adv.]** -- in a manner that acts as a clear and typical example of sth
2. **parenthetically** *[15]* **[adv.]** -- in a way that is additional to what you are saying in a speech or piece of writing
3. **parliamentarian** *[15]* **[n.]** -- a member of a parliament, especially one who is an expert on the formal rules/procedures of Parliament and takes active parts in debates || **[adj.]** -- relating to a parliament or its members
4. **parsimoniousness** *[16]* **[n.]** -- the quality or state of being not willing to spend money or to give/use much of sth [*synonyms:* meanness, niggardliness]
5. **particularities** *[15]* **[n.]** -- the special features, characteristics or details of sth
6. **peripatetically** *[15]* **[adv.]** -- in a manner that is characterized by traveling around to several different places, usually because of your job
7. **perpendicularly** *[15]* **[adv.]** -- in a manner that is at an angle of 90° to a horizontal line or surface
8. **perspicaciously** *[15]* **[adv.]** -- in a manner that is characterized by having or showing keen understanding [*synonym:* perceptively]
9. **pessimistically** *[15]* **[adv.]** -- in a manner that shows a tendency to see, feel or think the bad or negative aspects of things or is characterized by the belief that the bad or unsuccessful will happen [*synonyms:* cynicism, negativity]
10. **pharmaceutically** *[16]* **[adv.]** -- in a manner that is according to the methods of preparing medicines
11. **philanthropically** *[17]* **[adv.]** -- in a manner that is characterized by the practice or desire of helping the poor, sick and needy people, especially by donating money in large amounts
12. **philosophically** *[15]* **[adv.]** -- *(a).* in a manner that is connected with or relating to philosophers or philosophy (= a set of beliefs or values) | *(b).* in a manner that is characterized by staying calm and not getting upset,

disturbed or worried about difficult or disappointing situations [*synonym:* stoically]

13. **phosphorescence** *[15]* [n.] -- a kind of glow or weak/soft light that is produced in the dark without using noticeable heat

14. **phosphorescently** *[16]* [adv.] -- in a manner that produces a small amount of light in the dark

15. **photographically** *[16]* [adv.] -- in a way that is connected with, is used for, or is produced by photography

16. **phototypesetter** *[15]* [n.] -- a machine for film-setting or phototypesetting

17. **physiologically** *[15]* [adv.] -- in a manner that relates to the functions of living organisms and their parts

18. **postoperatively** *[15]* [adv.] -- relating to the period of time after a surgical medical procedure

19. **praiseworthiness** *[16]* [n.] -- the quality of deserving approval, admiration and respect

20. **prehistorically** *[15]* [adv.] -- in a manner that relates to, or exists in times before written history

21. **preposterousness** *[16]* [n.] -- the quality of being extremely unreasonable, senseless and foolish [*synonyms:* absurdity, outlandishness]

22. **presumptuousness** *[16]* [n.] -- the fact, state or quality of being rude or too confident in a way that involves sth without having any right or authority ignoring respect for other people [*synonyms:* arrogance, conceitedness]

23. **pretentiousness** *[15]* [n.] -- *(a).* an attempt to appear or sound cleverer, more important, intelligent, significant, etc. than you are in order to impress other people | *(b)*; an attempt to be sth that you are not, in order to impress || [*synonyms:* ostentatious, pompous]

24. **pretentiousness** *[15]* [n.] -- the state or quality of trying to appear important, intelligent, influential, clever, etc. or be sth that you are not, in order to impress other people

25. **preternaturally** *[15]* [adv.] -- in a manner that does not seem usual and cannot be explained by natural laws

26. **probabilistically** *[17]* [adv.] -- in a way that is based on or relates to the likelihood of the occurrence of sth

27. **problematically** *[15]* [adv.] -- in a way that has or causes many problems or difficulties and therefore difficult to solve

28. **procrastination** *[15]*) [n.] -- the act of delaying doing sth that you should do, till another day or time, usually because you do not want to do it, often because it is boring or unpleasant [*synonyms:* deferment, postponement]

29. **prognostication** *[15]* [n.] -- a statement that is made by sb to tell what is going to happen in the future [*synonym:* prediction]

30. **programmability** *[15]* [n.] -- the quality or state of being capable of being changed within hardware and software

31. **programmatically** *[16]* [adv.] -- in a way that is connected with or follows a plan or uses a particular method

32. **progressiveness** *[15]* [n.] -- the state or quality of favoring new ideas, reforms, improvements

33. **proportionality** *[15]* [n.] -- the principle or belief that sth, especially a punishment should be in proper balance as to degree, severity, etc. of an action

34. **proportionately** *[15]* [adv.] -- in a manner that is of the right size, number, amount or degree in relation to or in comparison with sth else

35. **propositionally** *[15]* [adv.] -- relating to statements or problems that need to be resolved or proven to be accurate or false

36. **psychiatrically** *[15]* [adv.] -- in a way that involves or relates to mental illness or its study

37. **psychoanalytical** *[16]* [adj.] -- relating to the method of treating mental disorders using a set of psychological theories and therapeutic techniques

38. **psychoanalytically** *[18]* [adv.] -- in a way that uses or relates to psychoanalysis (=encouraging someone to talk about their prior

experiences and feelings to understand anxieties and sentiments they were not aware of is a treatment method for mental health issues)

39. **psychologically** *[15]* [adv.] -- in a way that relates to the human mind and feelings

40. **psychometrically** *[16]* [adv.] -- in a matter that is designed to show sb's personality, mental ability, and thought processes, etc.

41. **psychopathology** *[15]* [n.] -- *(a).* the scientific study of mental disorders, that includes their causes, process, classification, treatment, etc. | *(a).* a disorder that affects mind or behavior or sb

42. **psychosomatically** *[17]* [adv.] -- in a manner that is caused by anxiety, stress and worry and not by an injury or infection

43. **punctiliousness** *[15]* [n.] -- the quality, state or fact of being extremely attentive or careful to behave correctly or to perform your duties exactly as they should be done [*synonyms:* assiduousness, meticulousness, scrupulousness]

44. **pyrotechnically** *[15]* [adv.] -- in a manner that relates to, resembles, or suggests fireworks

<u>15- to 18-Letter Words -- Q</u>

1. **quarrelsomeness** *[15]* [n.] -- the quality of being argumentative in nature

2. **questionability** *[15]* [n.] -- the quality or state of being unlikely to be completely acceptable, correct, honest, true or reasonable [*synonyms:* dubiousness, unlikelihood]

3. **quintessentially** *[16]* [adv.] -- *(a).* in a manner that shows the perfect, ideal or typical example of sth | *(b).* in a manner that shows the most important features or qualities of sth [*synonym:* essentially]

<u>15- to 18-Letter Words</u> -- R

1. **reconcilability** *[15]* [n.] -- (of two different ideas, facts, etc.) the quality, state or fact of being true, or able to exist together, at the same time

2. **redistributable** *[15]* [adj.] -- permitted to share or give out things such as copies of software differently or again to make them available to other people

3. **remorselessness** *[15]* [n.] -- *(a).* the state or quality of being severe and showing no sadness, pity, compassion or guilt | *(b).* (of an unpleasant situation) the state or quality of being continued and getting worse and worse

4. **repetitious**ness *[15]* [n.] -- the quality, state or fact of involving sth, especially unnecessary and boring thing that is expressed or happening in the same way over and over again

5. **reprehensibility** *[16]* [n.] -- the quality or state of being morally wrong and deserving blame, criticism or condemnation [*synonyms:* culpability, liability]

6. **representational** *[16]* [adj.] -- *(a).* (especially of a style of art or painting) trying to show things as they are normally seen physically | *(b).* involving the act of representing sb/sth

7. **representatively** *[16]* [adv.] -- in a manner that is typical of others in a larger group of people or things [*synonym:* characteristically]

8. **resourcefulness** *[15]* [n.] -- the state, quality or fact of having the ability or skill to find and use quick, creative, clever and effective ways to solve problems/difficulties, etc. or achieve your goal [*synonym:* ingenuity]

9. **retrospectively** *[15]* [adv.] -- *(a).* in a manner that relates to, thinks about or deals with events, situations, etc. that occurred in the past | *(b).* (of a new law, rule, etc.) in a manner that is intended to take effect from a particular date in the past

10. **revolutionarily** *[15]* [adv.] -- in a way that relates to a big change in sth, especially in the way a country is governed

11. **ritualistically** *[15]* [adv.] -- in a way that involves, is connected with or is like a set of fixed actions, especially ones performed as part of a ceremony

<u>15-</u> <u>to</u> <u>18-Letter</u> <u>Words</u> -- S

1. **sanctimoniously** *[15]* **[adv.]** -- in a manner that suggests you feel you are better and morally superior to other people, shown by your action or behavior [*synonyms:* self-righteously, superciliously]

2. **sanctimoniousness** *[17]* **[n.]** -- the quality, state or fact of trying to show you are better and morally superior to other people [*synonym:* self-righteousness, superciliousness]

3. **schizophrenically** *[17]* **[adv.]** -- *(a).* in a way that changes completely from one thing state to another, without any obvious reason or pattern | *(b).* in a way that relates to or having schizophrenia (=a chronic, severe mental disorder that affects how a person thinks, acts, behaves, expresses emotions, and perceives reality)

4. **scintillatingly** *[15]* **[adv.]** -- in a manner that is lively, exciting, and clever

5. **semiconsciously** *[15]* **[adv.]** -- in a manner that is characterized by only partly attentive and not fully awake

6. **semiprofessional** *[16]* **[adj.]** -- actively engaged in an activity, such as in a sport for pay but not on a full-time basis || **[n.]** -- a person who is engaged in an activity, such as in a sport for pay but not on a full-time basis

7. **semiprofessionally** *[18]* **[adv.]** -- in a manner that is characterized by being similar to but needing less ability, knowledge, and judgment than professional work

8. **semitransparent** *[15]* **[adj.]** -- allowing some visibility but obscured

9. **sententiousness** *[15]* **[n.]** -- the quality, state or fact of making an effort to appear to be sound important, impressive, intelligent or wise, especially by expressing moral opinions, in a way that is annoying

10. **serendipitously** *[15]* **[adv.]** -- in a manner that happens or is found by chance

11. **serviceableness** *[15]* **[n.]** -- the quality or state of being able to provide good service

12. **shortsightedness** *[16]* **[n.]** -- *(a).* a condition of the eye that involves the inability to see objects in a clear way unless they are relatively close to the eyes | *(b).* lack of imaginative power about how an action will affect the future [*synonym:* thoughtlessness]

13. **simultaneousness** *[16]* **[n.]** -- the quality or fact of being happened, existed, operated or done at exactly the same time as sth else

14. **socialistically** *[15]* **[adv.]** -- in a manner that is in accordance with the principles of socialism (= an economic system in which the government or the public owns and controls the means of production)

15. **sophisticatedly** *[15]* **[adv.]** -- *(a).* in a manner that is characterized by having or showing a lot of worldly experience, knowledge and understanding, especially in relation to art, culture, literature, etc. [*synonym:* gracefully] | *(b).* (of an appliance, system, or technique) in a highly developed manner [*synonym:* complicatedly]

16. **sophisticatedly** *[15]* **[adv.]** -- in a manner that is characterized by having a good understanding of the way people behave and a good knowledge of social trends or culture

17. **stereographically** *[17]* **[adv.]** -- in a manner that pertains to, or defines the shape of a solid body (such as the earth) on a plane

18. **stereotypically** *[15]* **[adv.]** -- in a manner that is based on fixed thoughts, ideas or images of a particular type of person or thing which are often untrue in reality

19. **straightforward** *[15]* **[adj.]** -- *(a).* simple or easy to do or to understand [*synonym:* uncomplicated] | *(b).* (of a person or their behavior) clear, frank, simple, honest and open

20. **straightforwardly** *[17]* **[adv.]** -- *(a).* in a manner that is simple or easy to do or to understand [*synonym:* uncomplicatedly] | *(b).* in a manner that is clear, frank, simple, honest and open

21. **substitutability** *[16]* **[n.]** -- the ability of goods or services to be replaced or exchanged by equivalent another similar good or service

22. **superciliousness** *[16]* **[n.]** -- the quality, state or fact of behaving in a manner that shows you think you are better, more important than other

people and ignores their opinions, beliefs or ideas, etc. [*synonyms:* arrogance, disdain, haughtiness]

23. **superheavyweight** *[16]* **[n.]** -- a boxer, wrestler or weight lifter who competes in the heaviest class

24. **superintendence** *[15]* **[n.]** -- the arrangement or management of activity in a particular department, office, or organization [*synonym:* supervision]

25. **superstitiously** *[15]* **[adv.]** -- in a manner that involves a belief that has no scientific basis; in a manner that is characterized by the belief that a particular event leads to good or bad luck [*synonyms:* irrationally, illogically]

26. **surreptitiously** *[15]* **[adv.]** -- in a manner that is characterized by doing, making, obtaining, etc. secretly or quickly so that other people cannot notice [*synonyms:* clandestinely, furtively, sneakily]

27. **surreptitiousness** *[17]* **[n.]** -- the quality of being obtained, done, made, etc. in a secret or unauthorized way [*synonym:* trickery]

28. **susceptibleness** *[15]* **[n.]** -- the quality, state or fact of being easily affected by sth

29. **sympathetically** *[15]* **[adv.]** -- in a way that shows that you care about sb's problems or support sb's views [*synonyms:* compassionately, considerately]

30. **symptomatically** *[15]* **[adv.]** -- in a manner that shows the existence of a problem or bad situation

31. **synchronization** *[15]* **[n.]** -- *(a).* the fact of sth occurring at the same time or moving, operating, working, etc. at the same speed as sth [*synonym:* harmonization] | *(b).* an act of adjusting a timepiece to show the same time as another

32. **synergistically** *[15]* **[adv.]** -- in a manner that makes use of the extra energy, power, success, etc. that is achieved by two or more people, companies or elements working together

33. **systematization** *[15]* **[n.]** -- an act of arranging, organizing or regulating sth in accordance with a particular system, order, etc. [*synonym:* standardization]

15- to 18-Letter Words -- T

1. **technologically** *[15]* [adv.] -- in a manner that relates to or involves technology

2. **temperamentally** *[15]* [adv.] -- in a manner that is characterized by having a tendency to change your behavior or mood very suddenly, or becoming angry easily

3. **tempestuousness** *[15]* [n.] -- the quality of being full of strong emotions; the quality of being very stormy [*synonym:* turbulence]

4. **tendentiousness** *[15]* [n.] -- the fact of expressing, supporting or intending to promote a particular cause, or opinion strongly, that people are likely to disagree with

5. **terminologically** *[16]* [adv.] -- in a way that relates to the unique words or expressions used in a specific subject or activity

6. **thermostatically** *[16]* [adv.] -- in a manner that is connected with or uses a thermostat

7. **thoughtlessness** *[15]* [n.] -- the quality or fact of not caring about the likely effects of your words, actions or behavior on other people [*synonym:* inconsideration]

8. **tintinnabulation** *[16]* [n.] -- a ringing or tinkling sound of bells

9. **topographically** *[16]* [adv.] -- in a manner that relates to the physical appearance such as the position or rivers or mountains of an area of land

10. **totalitarianism** *[15]* [n.] -- a form of a political system of government where there is only one political party that has complete or unrestricted power and control over the people of the country

11. **toxicologically** *[15]* [adv.] -- in a manner that relates to the scientific study of the characteristics and effects of poisons

12. **transcendentally** *[16]* **[adv.]** -- in a manner that is beyond the understanding of scientific knowledge, reason, etc., especially in a matter of religion or spirituality [*synonym:* heavenly]

13. **transcendentally** *[16]* **[adv.]** -- in a manner that is very unique, strange, and cannot be understood in normal ways, especially in a religious or spiritual way

14. **transcontinental** *[16]* **[adj.]** -- (of a railway line, etc.) crossing a continent

15. **transferability** *[15]* **[n.]** -- the quality of being able to be transported, transmitted or removed from one place, person, etc., to another

16. **transferability** *[15]* **[n.]** -- the quality of being conveyed or passed from one place, person, etc., to another [*synonym:* exchangeability]

17. **transfiguration** *[15]* **[n.]** -- a complete change in the form or appearance of a person or thing into a more beautiful, positive or spiritual [*synonyms:* metamorphosis, transformation]

18. **transformational** *[16]* **[adj.]** -- relating to, characterized by, or concerned with producing a complete, major and positive change or improvement in a situation or in the appearance, character or form of sb/sth

19. **translatability** *[15]* **[n.]** -- the quality of being able to be put into another form, style or language without making fundamental changes

20. **transliteration** *[15]* **[n.]** -- the process of writing or printing words or letters using the closest corresponding letters of a different alphabet or language

21. **transmissibility** *[16]* **[n.]** -- (of a disease, characteristic or trait, etc.) the quality of being able to be transmitted or passed on from one person or organism to another

22. **transmogrification** *[18]* **[n.]** -- a complete, magical, strange or surprising change in sb/sth [*synonym:* transformation]

23. **transplantation** *[15]* **[n.]** -- *(a).* the process of replacing a damaged living tissue, organ, skin, etc. with one from another person animal, part of the body, etc. | *(b).* the process of moving a growing plant and planting it somewhere else | *(c).* the process of moving sb/sth to a different environment, place or situation

24. **transportability** *[16]* **[n.]** -- the quality of being able to be carried or moved from place to place on a truck, train, plane, ship, etc.

25. **treacherousness** *[15]* **[n.]** -- the quality of being dangerous, untrustworthy or deceitful

26. **trigonometrically** *[17]* **[adv.]** -- in a manner that relates to, or is in accordance with trigonometry (= a branch of mathematics that deals with the relationship between the sides and angles of triangles)

27. **troubleshooting** *[15]* **[n.]** -- an act or the process of solving problems in an organization | an act or the process of correcting technical faults in a machine or electrical system

28. **troublesomeness** *[15]* **[n.]** -- the quality, state or fact of causing annoyance, difficulty, pain, trouble, etc. over a long period of time [*synonyms:* annoyance, irritation]

29. **trustworthiness** *[15]* **[n.]** -- the quality or fact of being able to be relied on as good, honest, sincere, etc. [*synonyms:* dependability, uprightness]

15- to 18-Letter Words -- U

1. **unacceptability** *[15]* [n.] -- the quality or state of not being able to be approved of or allowed

2. **unaccountability** *[16]* [n.] -- *(a).* the quality of not being responsible for sth | *(b).* the quality of being impossible to be understood

3. **unadventurously** *[15]* [adv.] -- in a manner that is characterized by not being willing to try new or difficult things

4. **unambiguousness** *[15]* [n.] -- the quality of being completely clear [*synonym:* lucidity]

5. **unapologetically** *[16]* [adv.] -- in a manner that is characterized by not accepting mistakes or expressing regret or shame that you are sorry about sth, even when you should

6. **unceremoniously** *[15]* [adv.] -- in a rough, sudden and rude manner [*synonym:* brusquely]

7. **unchallengeable** *[15]* [adj.] -- that cannot be disputed, opposed, questioned, or defeated [*synonyms:* indisputable, unassailable]

8. **unchallengeable** *[15]* [adj.] -- that is impossible to be challenged, disputed, opposed, questioned or defeated [*synonyms:* indisputable, unassailable]

9. **unchangeableness** *[16]* [n.] -- the state or quality of being unchangeable on consistent

10. **uncharacteristic** *[16]* [adj.] -- not typical of particular sb/sth of sb's usual behavior [*synonyms:* aberrant, atypical]

11. **uncommunicative** *[15]* [adj.] -- (of a person) unwilling to provide information, give opinions or talk to other people [*synonyms:* reserved, taciturn, tight-lipped]

12. **uncommunicatively** *[17]* [adv.] -- (of a person) in a manner that is characterized by an unwillingness to talk to other people or give opinions or disclose information [*synonyms:* reservedly, taciturnly]

13. **uncomplainingly** *[15]* **[adv.]** -- in a manner that is characterized by the willingness to face difficult, boring or unpleasant situations without complaining or becoming angry or sad

14. **uncomplicatedly** *[15]* **[adv.]** -- in a manner that is not difficult to understand or deal with

15. **uncomplimentary** *[15]* **[adj.]** -- rude or insulting [*synonym:* derogatory]

16. **uncomprehending** *[15]* **[adj.]** -- (of a person) showing or having an inability to understand a situation or what is happening [*synonym:* inane]

17. **uncomprehendingly** *[17]* **[adv.]** -- (of a person) in a manner that shows or has an inability to understand a situation or what is happening [*synonyms:* inanely, perplexedly]

18. **uncompromisingly** *[16]* **[adv.]** -- in a manner that shows an unwillingness to change your opinions about sb/sth or your behavior [*synonyms:* inflexibly, unbendingly]

19. **unconditionally** *[15]* **[adv.]** -- in a manner that is complete and not limited by requirements, conditions, etc. in any way

20. **unconstitutionally** *[18]* **[adv.]** -- in a manner that is not allowed by the governmental or official rules

21. **unconventionality** *[17]* **[n.]** -- the quality or fact of being different and often interesting from what is usual, formal, normal or acceptable practices, standards, rules, etc. [*synonym:* eccentricity]

22. **unconventionally** *[16]* **[adv.]** -- in a manner that is different and often interesting from what is usual, formal, normal or acceptable practices, standards, rules, etc. [*synonym:* unorthodoxly]

23. **uncooperatively** *[15]* **[adv.]** -- in a manner that shows an unwillingness to do what sb wants or asks for

24. **uncoordinatedly** *[15]* **[adv.]** -- In a badly planned or organized manner

25. **undemocratically** *[16]* [adv.] -- in a manner that is against or not according to the principles or values of democracy

26. **undemonstrative** *[15]* [adj.] -- tending to not show or express feelings of affection openly [*synonym:* restrained]

27. **undemonstratively** *[17]* [adv.] -- in a manner that is characterized by not showing emotion or feelings in a freely and openly

28. **underachievement** *[16]* [n.] -- the fact or state of failing to do as well as expected or supposed to, especially in schoolwork; the fact or state of not utilizing your full potential

29. **underdevelopment** *[18]* [n.] -- the state or quality of being developed too less that is characterized by underutilization of resources or having a low standard of living

30. **underemployment** *[15]* [n.] -- the state of not having enough paid work available to do as a job for a worker; the state of not having enough quality paid work available to do as a job for skilled people

31. **underestimation** *[15]* [n.] -- an estimate that is too low

32. **underinvestment** *[15]* [n.] -- (especially of companies) an insufficient amount of investment because there is a low expectation of profit

33. **undernourishment** *[16]* [n.] -- the state or fact of being in bad health or condition because of having insufficient food or lack of nutritious substances that are required for good health and condition [*synonym:* malnourishment]

34. **underperformance** *[16]* [n.] -- *(a).* the fact of being not as successful or well as other things of the same kind or as was expected | *(b).* (of shares, etc.) the fact of being increased in value that is less than expected

35. **underprivileged** *[15]* [adj.] -- [usually before noun] (of a person) lacking the money, education, rights, opportunities, or standard of living than most people in society [*synonym:* deprived] || [n.] -- (the

underprivileged) people who lack the money, education, rights, opportunities, the standard of living than most people in society

36. **underrepresented** *[16]* **[adj.]** -- inadequately or insufficiently represented in numbers in a group, organization, etc.

37. **understandability** *[17]* **[n.]** -- the quality or state of being able to be understood

38. **understandingly** *[15]* **[adv.]** -- in a manner that is characterized by the knowledge, skill and ability to judge or evaluate a particular situation or subject

39. **underutilization** *[16]* **[n.]** -- the fact of not using sth fully or sufficiently

40. **undifferentiated** *[16]* **[adj.]** -- having parts that you cannot tell apart; not split or divided into different elements, parts or sections

41. **undistinguished** *[15]* **[adj.]** -- without any interesting, successful or attractive characteristics or features [*synonyms:* ordinary, unremarkable]

42. **unenforceability** *[16]* **[n.]** -- the quality or state of not being able to be enforced or imposed

43. **unexceptionable** *[15]* **[adj.]** -- *(a).* not offering any basis or reason for criticism or objection | *(b).* not original, exciting or very new

44. **unexceptionably** *[15]* **[adv.]** -- in a manner that is characterized by not giving any reason for criticism

45. **unexceptionally** *[15]* **[adv.]** -- in a manner that is not unusual or extraordinary

46. **ungrammatically** *[15]* **[adv.]** -- in a manner that is not regarded as correct according to rules of grammar by native speakers of the language

47. **unimaginatively** *[15]* **[adv.]** -- in a manner that is characterized by being unable to think of new or original things

48. **unintelligently** *[15]* **[adv.]** -- in a manner that has no or small amount of intelligence

49. **unintelligibility** *[17]* **[n.]** -- the quality, state or fact of being impossible or extremely difficult to understand or comprehend [*synonyms:* incomprehensibility, incoherence]

50. **unintentionally** *[15]* **[adv.]** -- in a manner that is not planned [*synonym:* inadvertently]

51. **uninterestingly** *[15]* **[adv.]** -- in a manner that is without interest, attention, curiosity or excitement

52. **uninterruptedly** *[15]* **[adv.]** -- in a manner that is without any pauses or interruptions in time or space

53. **unmanageability** *[15]* **[n.]** -- the quality or state of being impossible to deal with or manage

54. **unobjectionable** *[15]* **[adj.]** -- (especially of behavior or especially language) not causing or likely to cause objection or offense [*synonyms:* inoffensive, innocuous]

55. **unobjectionably** *[15]* **[adv.]** -- (especially of behavior or especially language) in a manner that is not causing or likely to cause objection or offense [*synonyms:* inoffensively, innocuously]

56. **unprecedentedly** *[15]* **[adv.]** -- in a manner that has never happened, never existed, been done or been known in the past

57. **unpredictability** *[16]* **[n.]** -- *(a).* the state or quality of not being able to be guessed or expected before it happens because it involves sudden, unreasonable changes, or depends on too many different things or factors | *(b).* (of a person) the state or quality of changing the behavior often and suddenly

58. **unpremeditatedly** *[16]* **[adv.]** -- (of an act, remark, crime, etc.) in a manner that is not thought out or planned in advance [*synonym:* spontaneously]

59. **unprepossessing** *[15]* **[adj.]** -- not making a good or strong impression [*synonyms:* unattractive, uninviting]

60. **unpretentiously** *[15]* **[adv.]** -- in a manner that does not try to appear more special, clever, intelligent, smart, important, etc. than the reality [*synonym:* modestly]

61. **unpretentiousness** *[17]* **[n.]** -- the quality of being plain, simple and sincere [*synonyms:* ingenuousness, modesty]

62. **unprofessionally** *[16]* **[adv.]** -- in a manner that falls short of the expected standards of conduct for sb performing a specific job

63. **unprofitability** *[15]* **[n.]** -- the state or quality of not producing much gain, result, etc.

64. **unpronounceable** *[15]* **[adj.]** -- (of a word or name) almost impossible or too difficult to say

65. **unquestioningly** *[15]* **[adv.]** -- in a manner that is accepted, done or given without asking questions, or expressing doubt, disagreement, hesitation, etc.

66. **unrealistically** *[15]* **[adv.]** -- in a way that is not based on facts about a situation, or is unlikely to be successful

67. **unreasonableness** *[16]* **[n.]** -- *(a).* the quality or fact of not being based on good judgment | *(b).* the quality or fact expecting too much then it is fair or acceptable || [*synonym:* irrationality]

68. **unreconstructed** *[15]* **[adj.]** -- [only before noun] (of people and their beliefs or opinions) not having changed according to modern times

69. **unrepeatability** *[15]* **[n.]** -- (of an event, price, etc.) the state or quality of being unable to happen again

70. **unrepresentative** *[16]* **[adj.]** -- not having a set of characteristics of a particular class, group, society, etc. [*synonym:* untypical]

71. **unrepresentatively** *[18]* **[adv.]** -- in a manner that is not typical or usual of a larger group of people or things

72. **unresponsiveness** *[16]* [n.] -- the quality of not reacting, replying or responding to a question, demand, request, etc satisfactorily

73. **unsatisfactorily** *[16]* [adv.] -- in a manner that is not as good as it should be, and therefore considered unacceptable [*synonym:* disappointingly]

74. **unscrupulousness** *[16]* [n.] -- the quality, state or fact of not being honest, moral or fair in order to get what you want [*synonym:* crookedness]

75. **unselfconscious** *[15]* [adj.] -- behaving naturally or sincerely without worrying about what other people think of you

76. **unselfconsciously** *[17]* [adv.] -- in a manner that involves natural or sincere behavior without showing concern for what other people think of you

77. **unsentimentally** *[15]* [adv.] -- in a manner that is characterized by not being influenced by emotions or not giving too much importance to feelings

78. **unsophisticated** *[15]* [adj.] -- *(a).* not having or showing much experience of people and things from the world and social situations [*synonym:* unrefined] | *(b).* (of an appliance, system, or technique) not highly developed; simple and basic [*synonyms:* crude, primitive, uncomplicated]

79. **unsophisticatedly** *[17]* [adv.] -- *(a).* in a manner that has or shows much experience of people and things from the world and social situations | *(b).* (of an appliance, system, or technique) in a manner that is not highly developed; in a simple and basic way [*synonyms:* crudely, primitively, uncomplicatedly]

80. **unspectacularly** *[15]* [adv.] -- in a manner that is not exciting, impressive or extraordinary

81. **unspectacularly** *[15]* [adv.] -- in a manner that is not good, great, admiring or exciting, etc.

82. **unsportsmanlike** *[15]* [adj.] -- not behaving in a fair, kind, respectful, gracious and polite way, especially towards the opposing team or player in a sport or game

83. **unsubstantiated** *[15]* [adj.] -- (esp. of an argument or a claim) not proved or supported to be valid or true by evidence or facts [*synonyms:* unproven, unsupported]

84. **unsubstantiated** *[15]* [adj.] -- not supported or proved to be true or valid by evidence or facts [*synonyms:* unproven, unsupported]

85. **unsympathetically** *[17]* [adv.] -- *(a).* in a manner that does not feel, show or express any sympathy about sb's suffering, problems, etc. [*synonyms:* indifferently, insensitively, uncaringly] | *(b).* in a manner that does not support or approve an idea, action or aim, etc.; in a manner that is not in agreement with sth

86. **unsympathetically** *[17]* [adv.] -- *(a).* in a manner that indicates you are not feeling or showing care or understanding about someone's suffering [*synonyms:* insensitively, uncaringly] | *(b).* in a manner that is characterized by not supporting an aim, idea, policy, opinion, etc.; in a manner that is in disagreement with sth | *(c).* (of a person) in an unpleasant or unlikeable manner

87. **unsystematically** *[16]* [adv.] -- in a manner that is not organized according to a fixed plan or system [*synonym:* unmethodically]

88. **untranslatability** *[17]* [n.] -- the quality of being unable to be expressed or written down from one language to another language

89. **unwholesomeness** *[15]* [n.] -- the quality or state of being not good for sb physically, morally, or emotionally [*synonym:* vileness]

<u>15- to 18-Letter Words -- V - Z</u>

1. **wholeheartedness** *[16]* **[n.]** -- the quality or state of being completely devoted, enthusiastic, energetic, sincere, etc.; [*synonym:* dedication]

<u>ALSO NOTE:</u>

<u>19-LETTER WORDS</u>

2. **anthropocentrically** *[19]* **[adv.]** -- in a manner that involves the belief of humans being the most significant or central entity of the universes
3. **anthropomorphically** *[19]* **[adv.]** -- in a manner that involves the treatment of gods, animals or objects as if they have characteristics (in terms of appearance, behavior, etc.) of human beings
4. **chromatographically** *[19]* **[adv.]** -- in a manner that involves the laboratory technique for separation and analysis of a mixture of liquids or gases into the components
5. **cinematographically** *[19]* **[adv.]** -- in a manner that is characterized by specializations in the art and methods relating to the shooting of a film that involves shots, lighting, operating a camera, etc.
6. **contemporaneousness** *[19]* **[n.]** -- the state, quality, or property of happening, originating, living or existing in the same period of time [*synonym:* simultaneousness]
7. **counterintelligence** *[19]* **[n.]** -- secret activities conducted by a country to gather information in order to prevent another country from taking adverse action against its defense forces

8. **distinguishableness** *[19]* **[n.]** -- the quality of being easy to be recognized, noticed or identified as different from others of the same type

9. **electromagnetically** *[19]* **[adv.]** -- in a manner that has electrical characteristics or properties as well as the capacity to draw metal things

10. **extraterritoriality** *[19]* **[n.]** -- exemption or immunity from the application or jurisdiction of local law or tribunals

11. **impressionistically** *[19]* **[adv.]** -- in a manner that gives a general idea or view rather than particular facts or details

12. **incommensurableness** *[19]* **[n.]** -- the quality of being unable to be measured or compared by the same standard or measure

13. **incomprehensibility** *[19]* **[n.]** -- the state or fact of being impossible or extremely difficult to be understood [*synonyms:* inexplicability, unintelligibility]

14. **incontrovertibility** *[19]* **[n.]** -- the quality of being unable to be questioned and not worth arguing about [*synonym:* indisputability]

15. **interchangeableness** *[19]* **[n.]** -- the quality of being easily able to be used in place of each other

16. **interdenominational** *[19]* **[adj.]** -- existing, occurring, conducted between, or involving two or more religious denominations

17. **interdenominational** *[19]* **[adj.]** -- occurring between or among, involving or common to different churches or religious denominations

18. **straightforwardness** *[19]* **[n.]** -- *(a).* the state or quality of being simple or easy to do or to understand [*synonym:* uncomplicatedness] | *(b).* (of a person or their behavior) the state or quality of being clear, frank, simple, honest and open

19. **unselfconsciousness** *[19]* **[n.]** -- natural or sincere behavior without showing concern for what other people think of you

20. **unselfconsciousness** *[19]* **[n.]** -- the fact of always behaving in a natural, confident and sincere way

20-LETTER <u>WORDS</u>

1. **chemotherapeutically** *[20]* **[adv.]** -- in a manner that relates to the treatment of a disease, especially cancer by means of chemical substances that stop the growth of cancer cells
2. **incomprehensibleness** *[20]* **[n.]** -- the quality, state or fact of being impossible or extremely difficult to be understood [*synonyms:* inexplicableness, unintelligibility]
3. **incontrovertibleness** *[20]* **[n.]** -- the quality, state or fact of being undeniable and not worth arguing about
4. **internationalization (internationalisation)** *[20]* **[n.]** -- the process of bringing sth under the control, power or protection of many countries; the act or process becoming or making sth become international
5. **uncharacteristically** *[20]* **[adv.]** -- in a manner that is not typical of sb/sth or of sb's usual behavior [*synonyms:* aberrantly, atypically]

21-LETTER <u>WORDS</u>

1. **indistinguishableness** *[21]* **[n.]** -- the quality of being not easy to be recognized, noticed or identified as different from others of the same type

****

<u>About the Author</u>

Manik Joshi was born on January 26, 1979, at Ranikhet, a picturesque town in the Kumaon region of the Indian state of Uttarakhand. He is a permanent resident of the Sheeshmahal area of Kathgodam located in the city of Haldwani in the Kumaon region of Uttarakhand in India. He completed his schooling in four different schools. He is a science graduate in the ZBC – zoology, botany, and chemistry – subjects. He is also an MBA with a specialization in marketing. Additionally, he holds diplomas in "computer applications", "multimedia and web-designing", and "computer hardware and networking". During his schooldays, he wanted to enter the field of medical science; however, after graduation, he shifted his focus to the field of management. After obtaining his MBA, he enrolled in a computer education center; he became so fascinated with working on the computer that he decided to develop his career in this field. Over the following years, he worked at some computer-related full-time jobs. Following that, he became interested in Internet Marketing, particularly in domaining (business of buying and selling domain names), web design (creating websites), and various other online jobs. However, later he shifted his focus solely to self-publishing. Manik is a nature-lover. He has always been fascinated by overcast skies. He is passionate about traveling and enjoys solo travel most of the time rather than traveling in groups. He is actually quite a loner who prefers to do his own thing. He likes to listen to music, particularly when he is working on the computer. Reading and writing are definitely his favorite pastimes, but he has no interest in sports. Manik has always dreamed of a prosperous life and prefers to live a life of luxury. He has a keen interest in politics because he believes it is politics that decides everything else. He feels a sense of gratification sharing his experiences and knowledge with the outside world. However, he is an introvert by nature and thus gives prominence to only a few people in his personal life. He is not a spiritual man, yet he actively seeks knowledge about the metaphysical world; he is particularly interested in learning about life beyond death. In addition to writing academic/informational text and fictional content, he also maintains a personal diary. He has always had a desire to stand out from the crowd. He does not believe in treading the beaten path and avoids copying someone else's path to success. Two things he always refrains from are smoking and drinking; he is a teetotaler and very health-conscious. He usually wakes up before the sun rises. He starts his morning with meditation and exercise. Fitness is an integral and indispensable part of his life. He gets energized by solving complex problems. He loves himself the way he is and he loves the way he looks. He doesn't believe in following fashion trends. He dresses according to what suits him & what he is comfortable in. He believes in taking calculated risks. His philosophy is to expect the best but prepare for the worst. According to him, you can't succeed if you are unwilling to fail. For Manik, life is about learning from mistakes and figuring out how to move forward.

Amazon Author Page of Manik Joshi:
https://www.amazon.com/author/manikjoshi
Email: manik85joshi@gmail.com

BIBLIOGRAPHY

(A). SERIES TITLE: "ENGLISH DAILY USE" *[40 BOOKS]*

01. How to Start a Sentence
02. English Interrogative Sentences
03. English Imperative Sentences
04. Negative Forms In English
05. Learn English Exclamations
06. English Causative Sentences
07. English Conditional Sentences
08. Creating Long Sentences In English
09. How to Use Numbers In Conversation
10. Making Comparisons In English
11. Examples of English Correlatives
12. Interchange of Active and Passive Voice
13. Repetition of Words
14. Remarks In the English Language
15. Using Tenses In English
16. English Grammar- Am, Is, Are, Was, Were
17. English Grammar- Do, Does, Did
18. English Grammar- Have, Has, Had
19. English Grammar- Be and Have
20. English Modal Auxiliary Verbs
21. Direct and Indirect Speech
22. Get- Popular English Verb
23. Ending Sentences with Prepositions
24. Popular Sentences In English
25. Common English Sentences
26. Daily Use English Sentences
27. Speak English Sentences Every Day
28. Popular English Idioms and Phrases
29. Common English Phrases
30. Daily English- Important Notes
31. Collocations In the English Language
32. Words That Act as Multiple Parts of Speech (Part 1)
33. Words That Act as Multiple Parts of Speech (Part 2)
34. Nouns In the English Language
35. Regular and Irregular Verbs
36. Transitive and Intransitive Verbs

37. 10,000 Useful Adjectives In English
38. 4,000 Useful Adverbs In English
39. 20 Categories of Transitional Expressions
40. How to End a Sentence

****

(B). SERIES TITLE: "ENGLISH WORD POWER" *[30 BOOKS]*

01. Dictionary of English Synonyms
02. Dictionary of English Antonyms
03. Homonyms, Homophones and Homographs
04. Dictionary of English Capitonyms
05. Dictionary of Prefixes and Suffixes
06. Dictionary of Combining Forms
07. Dictionary of Literary Words
08. Dictionary of Old-fashioned Words
09. Dictionary of Humorous Words
10. Compound Words In English
11. Dictionary of Informal Words
12. Dictionary of Category Words
13. Dictionary of One-word Substitution
14. Hypernyms and Hyponyms
15. Holonyms and Meronyms
16. Oronym Words In English
17. Dictionary of Root Words
18. Dictionary of English Idioms
19. Dictionary of Phrasal Verbs
20. Dictionary of Difficult Words
21. Dictionary of Verbs
22. Dictionary of Adjectives
23. Dictionary of Adverbs
24. Dictionary of Formal Words
25. Dictionary of Technical Words
26. Dictionary of Foreign Words
27. Dictionary of Approving & Disapproving Words
28. Dictionary of Slang Words
29. Advanced English Phrases
30. Words In the English Language

****

(C). SERIES TITLE: "WORDS IN COMMON USAGE" *[10 BOOKS]*

01. How to Use the Word "Break" In English
02. How to Use the Word "Come" In English
03. How to Use the Word "Go" In English
04. How to Use the Word "Have" In English
05. How to Use the Word "Make" In English
06. How to Use the Word "Put" In English
07. How to Use the Word "Run" In English
08. How to Use the Word "Set" In English
09. How to Use the Word "Take" In English
10. How to Use the Word "Turn" In English

****

(D). SERIES TITLE: "WORDS BY NUMBER OF LETTERS" *[10 BOOKS]*

01. Dictionary of 4-Letter Words
02. Dictionary of 5-Letter Words
03. Dictionary of 6-Letter Words
04. Dictionary of 7-Letter Words
05. Dictionary of 8-Letter Words
06. Dictionary of 9-Letter Words
07. Dictionary of 10-Letter Words
08. Dictionary of 11-Letter Words
09. Dictionary of 12- to 14-Letter Words
10. Dictionary of 15- to 18-Letter Words

****

(E). SERIES TITLE: "ENGLISH WORKSHEETS" *[10 BOOKS]*

01. English Word Exercises (Part 1)
02. English Word Exercises (Part 2)
03. English Word Exercises (Part 3)
04. English Sentence Exercises (Part 1)
05. English Sentence Exercises (Part 2)
06. English Sentence Exercises (Part 3)
07. Test Your English
08. Match the Two Parts of the Words
09. Letter-Order In Words
10. Choose the Correct Spelling

www.ingramcontent.com/pod-product-compliance
Lightning Source LLC
Chambersburg PA
CBHW051914250726
48659CB00002B/640